1/24/14

To Keisha,
Live the Adventure
&
Love w/ Passion!

The 90-Minute Marriage Miracle

The Only Guide You Will Ever Need to Making Love Last

JEFF FORTE

BALBOA PRESS
A DIVISION OF HAY HOUSE

Copyright © 2013 Jeff Forte.

All rights reserved. No part of this book may be used or reproduced by any means, graphic, electronic, or mechanical, including photocopying, recording, taping or by any information storage retrieval system without the written permission of the publisher except in the case of brief quotations embodied in critical articles and reviews.

Balboa Press books may be ordered through booksellers or by contacting:

Balboa Press
A Division of Hay House
1663 Liberty Drive
Bloomington, IN 47403
www.balboapress.com
1-(877) 407-4847

Because of the dynamic nature of the Internet, any web addresses or links contained in this book may have changed since publication and may no longer be valid. The views expressed in this work are solely those of the author and do not necessarily reflect the views of the publisher, and the publisher hereby disclaims any responsibility for them.

The author of this book does not dispense medical advice or prescribe the use of any technique as a form of treatment for physical, emotional, or medical problems without the advice of a physician, either directly or indirectly. The intent of the author is only to offer information of a general nature to help you in your quest for emotional and spiritual well-being. In the event you use any of the information in this book for yourself, which is your constitutional right, the author and the publisher assume no responsibility for your actions.

Any people depicted in stock imagery provided by Thinkstock are models, and such images are being used for illustrative purposes only.
Certain stock imagery © Thinkstock.

Printed in the United States of America.

ISBN: 978-1-4525-8021-0 (sc)
ISBN: 978-1-4525-8019-7 (hc)
ISBN: 978-1-4525-8020-3 (e)

Library of Congress Control Number: 2013915000

Balboa Press rev. date: 08/30/2013

Table of Contents

Preface vii
Introduction xi
Breakthrough #1: Can You Handle the Truth? 1
Breakthrough #2: Check Your Vision 21
Breakthrough #3: Correct the Polarity 43
Breakthrough #4: A2—Attention and Appreciation 63
Breakthrough #5: Button Pushing Push Back 75
Breakthrough #6: Tropical Storms 99
Breakthrough #7: Me First or Maybe Not 129
Bonus #1: The Magic of Courage 147
Bonus #2: The Number One
              Relationship Destroyer 159
Bonus #3: Three Little Mistakes
              That Mess Up Any Marriage.................... 163
Bonus #4: Meet My Needs 167
Bonus #5: A Few Words on Affairs 175
Bonus #6: The Four Levels of Relationships 181
Bonus #7: Re-Ignite Passion Now 185
Summary 191
To Those Committed to Love 199
Marriage Fitness Membership Group 201

Preface

*Your marriage can suck or not,
you decide.*

How to get the most out of this book.

This book is called *The 90—Minute Marriage Miracle* because I have helped turn marriages on the edge of divorce back to love in that brief ninety minutes, and neither partner thought it was possible. It is also called *The 90-Minute Marriage Miracle* because in only about 90 minutes you will learn exactly what to do to make love last in your intimate relationship. The most impactful of all relationship success secrets that I use are right here. You will find this book to be incredibly useful and comprehensive as a guide to your marriage success.

This is in stark contrast to the years of traditional couples counseling, and hours and hours of searching that people go through, yet, still fail to shift their unhappy relationships. You will soon realize that suffering in any relationship is optional.

You are about to read the *Seven Breakthroughs* that I discovered on my path to relationship mastery. I believe that these are the most essential things to know if you want to repair, or improve your marriage immediately. Any poor, average, or even good relationship, has the potential to be great when the partners know what to do.

This book is based on my work helping to resolve interpersonal team conflict in the workplace as well as my seven years of private relationship coaching with clients. These ideas will provide you with the greatest payoff, in the shortest amount of time, for creating an amazing marriage.

You will also find *Seven Bonuses* that will take your understanding even deeper and shed much more light on how to quickly change any relationship dynamic. I know of no other single source place, to get this much highly valuable information. You will find these concepts easy to understand, and they can deliver immediate benefits when you put them into practice for yourself.

In my private practice I focus only on the tools and strategies that work right now. I want the biggest bang for the buck because I know personally about the pain of a marriage gone bad. So, for me time is of the essence. If these strategies can work for me, they can work for you as well.

Client results are important to me, and I have guaranteed my work with a 30-day, 100 percent money back guarantee for six years. So far, I've yet to be taken up on that offer. Why not find out today if it's possible to rescue your relationship?

There are also important questions to answer in the various chapters that will help you to get more clarity about your personal situation. It would be easy to overlook this part because answering these questions will require you to think a little deeper. You will get more out of this book if you take a few extra minutes to write your answers down, because understanding concepts intellectually isn't enough. What matters is how you relate this material to your own situation, and ultimately what you are willing to actually do about it.

I have included many actual client examples of relationships that were transformed, and only the names have been changed to protect their identities. The conversational tone of this book is direct and intended to get right to the heart of the issues.

Have some curiosity about what you are about to read. How might a particular idea influence your partner? How might it impact your relationship?

Curiosity can fill in the gaps between reading and applying the content of this book in your very own relationship.

Imagine how good it will feel if you turn your marriage into something magical.

Introduction

*You will never be truly happy until you get
the relationship part of your life right.*

My Story . . .

First a confession . . . I was a clueless man who screwed up my first marriage many years ago. How could I not? I not only had no clue, I had no plan. I also had lousy role models. Hopefully yours are better. My father moved out when I was fifteen, and my parents divorced. They argued and fought a lot. When I was eight years old, I wrote them a note asking them to stop. It didn't work. They continued and ultimately divorced. It hurt.

Because of the pain of my parents' divorce, the last thing I wanted for myself was to get divorced. I swore it would never happen. Not only did it happen, it was easy . . . far too easy. My marriage barely lasted five years. I didn't have any idea about what to do to make it work. I made so many big mistakes. I didn't even know what I didn't know about relationships.

A defining moment for me was in marriage counseling when I realized that I was going to get divorced and there was nothing I could do about it. The person giving us guidance was directing us down the road of no return . . . . divorce. There was to be no recovery, no reconciliation. The marriage was over. It didn't make any sense to me. The counselor wasn't interested in examining the cause of the problems between us, or getting to the core issues. There were no ideas about solving any problems. There was only blame and that it was time for us to go our separate ways.

Shortly after that experience, and a low point in my life, I made a decision that I was going to learn everything I could about relationships. I didn't want to ever make the same mistakes again, and I wasn't about to put myself through another marriage counseling experience. I had all the motivation I needed to figure it out.

This book will save you a lot of time, and help you to create real results for yourself if you apply what you are about to read. This work is based on my twelve years of resolving interpersonal conflict in the corporate world and my work with individuals and couples over the past seven years. I have trained, researched, and read extensively on the keys to successful relationships. More importantly, I have personally tested all of these ideas and concepts in my own marriage in order to figure out what works and doesn't work.

The results have paid off beyond my wildest imagination because I found a sense of freedom that I never knew existed. There is incredible peace of mind that comes from knowing exactly what to do to create the relationship you truly want. Imagine knowing that you can resolve any challenge that comes up in your relationship. You can have that freedom as well.

My experience of resolving interpersonal conflict came from managing offices of financial advisors, and working as a regional team development leader for high performing teams. This taught me a great deal about relationship dynamics. I learned how to resolve challenging situations quickly with stressed out, highly successful, type A personalities whose egos often clashed.

When the stakes are high and people are stressed, there's nothing like the practical urgency that conflict brings. It forces creativity to grow if you want to be successful. That clarity has been instrumental in my work helping fix marriages and struggling relationships.

Several of the ideas that you will read about came from my Strategic Intervention and Marriage Educator training with the Robbins-Madanes Center for Strategic Intervention. This book isn't based on theory. This knowledge comes from real work in my own marriage and being in the trenches with struggling couples where it's as real and raw as it gets.

You probably know that in any unfulfilled relationship people are angry. People are also hurt and very frustrated. These emotions can lead to significant levels of unhappiness between the couple. Sometimes the emotions have to come out. It's in those very real moments that these strategies have been put to the test and proven themselves over and over again.

I have heard many unhappy stories from both sides. I have seen many couples argue up close. As you realize, it can get pretty ugly when couples go at each other. Resolving these spontaneous disputes has forced me to dig deep into my own creativity. This valuable experience has resulted in the discovery of many simple solutions that work right now.

There was a moment when everything came together for me. In a flash of insight I realized that I had a recipe, or a blue print, that gave me total clarity on exactly what to do to make my own relationship amazing. I was blown away because it was so empowering. I knew in that moment I could handle any situation that came up in my marriage and fix it if I chose to . . . *that's right, if I chose to.* You will also get to choose.

I have been so liberated by what I have learned about relationships that I wanted to share it with others, so that they could avoid the pain I had experienced in the failure of my first marriage. Divorce is tougher than we think. It's brutal for everyone involved and the impact is far reaching to extended family and friends.

I married again, nine years after my divorce, and as of this writing, my wife and I have been together for fourteen truly happy years. Our amazing relationship seems to get better month after month. The passion and deep connection we share with each other continues to grow. This is not some *you're just lucky* situation. I personally use everything that you will read about in this book. I also use these strategies daily with private clients in my executive results coaching practice. These ideas work and they work fast every time.

But don't take my word for it. Here's your chance to discover the truth for yourself. And realize this; *understanding these concepts is not enough*. They will become real only when you apply them and experience what happens for yourself. That's the moment where true change begins, not when you finally get it intellectually.

Nothing will ever change because you think, "*Oh, I get it*, or *yeah, that makes sense.*" You have to actually do something if you want things to change. That's always your choice to make.

Imagine the freedom of knowing exactly what to do for any situation. Imagine the freedom to know that you can control many aspects of the relationship. I want you to experience that for yourself because so many people are suffering in their marriages and it's not necessary. Relationship stress is taking an emotional toll on the happiness of too many couples, and it's avoidable.

In my private coaching practice, I have saved, and turned, numerous marriages from the door step of divorce (even with attorneys involved) into happy successful relationships. Many times, I work with only one partner to shift the entire relationship. My experience is that the relationship dynamics can be changed immediately when you have one committed person.

What you are about to learn is surprisingly effective, but only if you apply it. These strategies can work no matter what's happened in your relationship including: affairs, lack of intimacy, lack of appreciation, lost trust and respect, disconnected communication, and even bitterness and resentment. I have experience with all of these issues and much more.

These strategies can potentially re-unite couples that have separated or divorced. Anything is possible when you stop making the simple mistakes that push each other away. When you add the strategies you are about to read, you have a very real chance for unbounded success. I would love to hear about your experience, email jeff@peakresultscoaching.com.

Your relationship is in your hands. You now have the power to shift it. The information to do it is right here. Will you?

Jeff Forte
www.peakresultscoaching.com
jeff@peakrsesultscoaching.com

#1 BREAKTHROUGH

Can You Handle the Truth?

High levels of career success and financial abundance, without a fulfilling relationship, create emptiness.

Can You Handle the Truth?

If your marriage is struggling, do you really want to save it? Do you even want a happy marriage? Not everyone does, not really. Let's find out. Rate your commitment level on a scale of 1-10 (10 meaning you are absolutely, totally committed to making your relationship work). So, what's your level of commitment? Not your partner's; what's *your* commitment? Give me a number, whatever number feels truthful to you. How committed are you? *Write it here ____.*

I ask this question to every person I see in my private practice. Based on my experience, very few people are committed at a level 9 or 10. Many people aren't even sure exactly what they want out of the relationship. This lack of clarity hurts them and keeps them from doing what they need to do in order for things to get better.

Many different factors limit people from doing what's necessary to sustain love and passion. For example; hurts from the past can hold people back, beliefs from previous relationship failures can act like barriers to new ideas; the experience of being rejected or feeling unworthy of love can influence someone's willingness to do anything at all. Every person has a story, but a new chapter can be written right here and right now.

"What if I commit and it doesn't work, or what if my partner doesn't change or what if I give everything and get nothing back." are what I frequently hear. Fear and uncertainty are common emotions when it comes to relationships. Those are all reasons to do very little.

Do you want to rethink your commitment level? If you answer totally honestly, how high is that number really? A value of 10 means that you are willing to do whatever it takes, anything, and everything. What would you do if you truly loved someone? What would you have done for him or her in the beginning of the marriage, compared to right now?

Now write your real commitment level here ____. Are your numbers the same?

It's important to tell yourself the truth. When you do, anything is possible. Knowing exactly where you stand can be a launching pad toward whatever you want. When you mislead yourself, you create limitations and blocks to success. It turns off your willingness without you even being aware of it.

What do you want your marriage to be like? Have you really thought about it? It's critically important that you be totally clear about what you want. Here's an example of why.

I have had both men and women as individual clients tell me that they wanted clarity about their marriage because they were having affairs. They didn't really want to fix or save their marriage. They simply wanted to know whether to stay married, or pursue a relationship with their affair partner, a huge difference. The optimal strategies used are not the same. You won't reconnect with your spouse while you are obsessively thinking of the fun and fantasy of an affair.

Sometimes people say, "I think I married the wrong person and now I'm stuck." Or "I'm tired of being taken for granted." Or "I just don't know what I want any more"

Or "My wife or husband has changed" There's always a reason something isn't working, but there are things to do right now to make things better. You need to know exactly what you are working towards if you want to create success. That's the only way it will happen. Are you clear about what you really want?

Brian

When I worked with Brian, he wanted the clarity of either staying in his marriage or leaving his wife to be with another woman a few states away. He glowed as he talked about the other woman and became bitter and negative as he talked about how angry and condescending his wife was. It was clear to me that he had already made up his mind to leave and was only looking for confirmation from me that it was the right thing to do.

My role is not to tell people what to do; it's to help them get total clarity and some real answers that will serve them immediately. It's all about helping them to get their result, not mine.

Reluctantly, he agreed to try some of my strategies, to get the clarity that he claimed to want. You will read about some of these specific ideas shortly. Brian called me four days later and told me that the ideas we had talked about were already working. He noticed an immediate shift in his wife's attitude toward him. Brian was very surprised.

The interesting thing was that he wasn't happy about it at all. He had hoped it wouldn't work. He really didn't want the marriage to succeed. He had already decided to leave, and this was ruining his plan. He was angry and frustrated with the realization that what I had told him was possible after all. Now he had to rethink his plans.

Ultimately, a few weeks later, he lost interest in the other woman much to his surprise and committed to his marriage. (How I helped that happen is a story for another book.) Because Brian had changed his approach, new life was breathed into the marriage. He began to fall in love with his wife all over again. You can fall in love with your partner all over again too, even if you think it's not possible. I see it happen often. The love is often buried under years of neglect and hurt.

What type of relationship is acceptable to you? For some people, staying together in the same house for the kids' sake is more important than leaving the stressed—out, unhappy environment they are creating for their family. For others, just getting along without conflict is enough to satisfy them, even though the relationship is lifeless; two roommates existing with each other. Not much of a recipe for love or even fun. Others are simply afraid of being alone, so they prefer to stay miserable with someone they really aren't all that interested in. What's your story? Do you still love your partner?

Life brings each of us plenty of challenges, so why should we bother to suffer needlessly in an empty relationship? It's your life; you get to decide how you want to experience it with the person you have chosen. Understand that there are things that can be done to shift the most troubled relationships, but most of us simply don't what they are. You are about to learn what I believe are the best of them.

One of the greatest gifts you can ever give to your children is the example of a happy, loving, deeply connected marriage. They will, of course, adopt many of your relationship strategies, whether they are beneficial or not. Imagine that for your children. Will it be happiness or hurt? Will it be success or sadness? Will it be giving up or getting it right?

I unknowingly adopted many unsuccessful strategies from my parents, despite my best intentions otherwise. We all take in pieces from our parental influence. What have you taken in that might not be serving you in your relationship?

What are you willing to do to get the results you want? Sometimes people give me the answers that think I want to hear. "I'll do anything", *or* "I'll do everything that needs to be done" or "I'll do whatever it takes". It's usually not true! They haven't really thought about it. You'll understand this better as you read a few of the other sections in this book. The reality is, there are lots of things that most people are unwilling to do to make the relationship work, or it would be working right now. Everyone has their reasons. What are yours?

If you are bitter, you are highly unlikely to want to give to your partner. If you feel you have been wronged, then maybe you have emotionally checked out. If you think it's entirely your partner's fault, then you might wait for them to change and do nothing. People have a long list of reasons why things can't work, or can they?

Do you have other priorities that come before the relationship? Some people put their work first, while others favor friends or family over their partner. Some people have hobbies that come first, and others put whatever they want to do for themselves ahead of the relationship. All of these can result in the unintended neglect of the significant other.

Do you know someone who always has to be right? Have you ever argued over something completely ridiculous?

People can fight with their partner for significance about who is more right. Most of these fights are about the most insignificant things. "I'm right." "No I'm more right" over who left the refrigerator door open; or dishes in the sink.

We make so many other things more important than the love of our life. It is all too easy for people to struggle with each other and feel hurt and empty.

The blunt reality is that the odds of success are not in your favor unless you make a decision to learn what works or get the right help. Relationships can be incredibly stressful when people are frustrated and upset. You very likely know people who are suffering. It's more common today for relationships to struggle rather than thrive.

Statistics—What's in the Numbers?

You may have heard all about the statistics of divorce. The numbers are very real. It's certainly not a pretty picture for many, but it can change for you quickly if you implement some of these ideas.

Here are a few of those ugly relationship facts for your consideration:

The Reality of Divorce Statistics? The National Center for Health Statistics data suggests that sixty percent of marriages between ages twenty to twenty-five divorce, and fifty percent of all other marriages divorce. The data on divorce statistics varies slightly from source to source, but it is widely accepted that at least half of marriages divorce.

According to The Forest Institute of Psychology more than sixty percent of all marriages divorce. That number is higher than you might think, because of the failure rate of second and third marriages. Third marriage failure rates are about seventy-three percent. Why? Because the same people still haven't figured it out. They haven't changed their approach. They continue to make the same mistakes over again, and are expecting a different result. If that's the definition of insanity, most of us must be a little insane. If you are in a second or third marriage, for your sake and everyone else involved, I hope I have your attention.

Children and Divorce I spent a few years earlier in my coaching career working with troubled youth, including suicidal teens, or those who were into cutting and burning themselves. Physically, self-inflicted pain was a just a way of escaping the emotional pain that they were going through. In my experience, they came from homes of divorced parents or troubled relationships.

The pain of divorce can be truly devastating on family members. According to the Journal of Marriage and Family, the children of divorce have much higher rates of divorce themselves when they marry. Will this be your legacy?

Is it better to live together and not marry? The numbers are not better here; forty-five percent of couples who live together break up and separate within the first five years according to the Annual Review of Sociology. By seven years that number is about sixty percent. This is not simply a marriage problem as some would have you believe.

The challenge is to take two people who fell in love, and to expect them to know how to communicate with each other under stress. To get these two people to sustain love and passion without any real understanding or thought about what that means and how to go about doing it. Some people figure it out. Those are the fortunate ones because most people never do.

Do you know any couples who are in amazing, loving, passionate, happy marriages? My guess is that the real number of truly happy marriages is around ten to fifteen percent. You too can be one of these rare couples who enjoy sharing your life in a successful, deeply connected, intimate relationship. However, that does require you to do something different. Nothing will get better for you unless you change what you are doing.

I'm curious, where did you learn how to create a happy, successful marriage? Did you learn about it in school? My University had a class on human sexuality that was wildly popular. The class was always filled. It was also the first class to sell out. Everyone is interested in sex. However, there was no class on how to make a relationship work; no class on what to do to handle partner communication and conflicts.

Today, finding someone for sex has never been easier, but it's an empty promise. You won't find long term fulfillment going from sex partner to sex partner. It can be fun and distracting and better than being alone, but it offers very limited rewards. More often than not it can be destructive on the subconscious self worth of the participants. The longer it goes on, the greater the emotional impact because people are inevitably alone after the physical fun.

Creating relationship success in my opinion, has never been more difficult because of our technology driven, hectic, and fast paced lives. We are all members of a self focused and self absorbed society with short attention spans looking for instant gratification. We are all receivers of the "it's all about me", media message. Our needs come first. We are self focused, self-absorbed, self-centered and often *self-ish*. What we personally want often matters more to us than our own best interests and those of the relationship.

Did you have great role models growing up or were your role models less than ideal? How would you describe the love and connection between your parents? Was the joy that they experienced every day together what you wanted for yourself?

It's easy to understand why most people simply don't know what to do to make each other happy in an intimate relationship. Will your children know what to do?

Are You Happy? Your overall life happiness and satisfaction is directly impacted by your ability to be in a successful relationship. In fact, a happy relationship is five times more important than any other ingredient in determining personal life happiness according to a recent worldwide survey of seventy-five thousand people reported in *The Normal Bar*. Finding and sustaining a partner to share your love and life with isn't just one of the keys to happiness, it's the Master Key. You cannot afford to mess this up. There's so much at stake here including your longevity. The scientific research shows that people who are married live longer than singles.

More Interesting Facts: According to the US Census Bureau, eighty percent of all divorce in college educated couples is initiated by the woman. If you are a man reading this, you should be a little concerned. Men are always caught off guard. Go figure. By the way, other surveys states up to one third of the women who initiate their divorce severely regret it shortly after, and wish to reconcile with their husbands. It's usually too late, and unfortunately, they experience the pain of regret which causes years of unhappiness.

Both men and women underestimate the emotional toll that divorce takes. This was absolutely true for me. I rationalized that everything would be fine and that it wasn't that big a deal. I was dead wrong. I went through the lowest point in my life and I never saw it coming.

Cheating and affairs. According to a survey from Indiana University in Bloomington, women have caught up with men in this category and now both cheat at about the same rates. A recent Huffington Post/YouGov poll actually has women cheating at a higher rate than men. This is not widely known. There are lots of common misconceptions about the reality of cheating. The number one affair website (who I will not name) has over twenty-one million anonymous members. Married men and women at an alarmingly increasing rate can point and click their way into affairs, with other married or single partners. You can just imagine the stress this is bringing into so many households. Suppressed guilt causes anger and short fuses.

I have yet to see an affair have a positive impact on marriage despite the current media mantra that suggests having an affair can spice up, or save the marriage.

The fleeting spontaneous adventures of pleasure seem like the perfect contrast to the day to day drudgery of living with a neglectful spouse. Unfortunately it's cotton candy and doesn't last. The spouse who is so neglectful is usually suffering from the same perception.

Here's an example of gender differences in cheating: According to this website, the top day for new membership signups for married women is the day after Valentine's Day. Why? Because the women were disappointed in whatever their partner did to celebrate that special day. This one day to celebrate love is an important day for women even when they deny that it is. But, it's the culmination of let-downs from disappointments over time, and the breach of the emotional threshold and it pushes women into affairs seeking to fill the emotional void.

In contrast, the top sign up day for men is the day after Father's Day. Why? Because the men feel unappreciated by their wives, and Father's Day is a day for men to feel valued. It's also a culmination event, this one from the heightening resentment that comes from being unappreciated over time. The absence of appreciation on that particularly important day is the trigger for men to rush into affairs, to also fill an emotional void.

Interestingly, in a long term followed survey by Dr. Jan Halper, of 4,100 men who left their marriage for another woman, less than three percent eventually married the other woman. This is a remarkably small number. Despite what people think initially when pursuing someone outside of the marriage, it's extremely rare that an affair partner will become a lifetime partner. It's mostly all an illusion or fantasy. You'll understand more as you read. Sorry, there are no long term statistics available about women who leave their marriages for the affair partners. My opinion is that their numbers would be about the same because today most other statistics between the sexes are extremely close.

The grass is not all that green on the other side of the fence. The relationships that people run to in order to escape their partners mostly fail. I wanted to give you this harsh reality because most people create a fantasy in their minds about the life that they will live when they leave their partner. If you are thinking about leaving your spouse for someone else, there is about a ninety-seven percent chance it won't work out long term with the other person. This is really rolling the dice. Does it make sense to bet on a ninety-seven percent loser?

Clearly reality doesn't correspond with the fantasy. Profound guilt and regret are usually the prevailing emotions people experience when the bubble bursts. This cripples people emotionally resulting in feelings that bounce back and forth between anger and depression.

Now it's your turn to think on paper about your situation. Remember, you will get much more out of this book if you take a few moments to answer the questions that you see. Give them the truthfulness you deserve.

Why do you want your marriage to work out?
_____
_____
_____

Is that a valid reason? ____Y/N Is it compelling enough for you to raise your commitment level? ____Y/N

What's at stake here beyond your own happiness, emotional and physical health, financial condition, overall life success, the impact on any children, friends and family? Did I miss anything? If so, write it here:

_____
_____
_____

Honestly describe the current state of your marriage?

_____
_____
_____
_____
_____

What's the biggest challenge in your marriage?

_____
_____
_____
_____
_____

What are you doing that make things in your relationship worse? (A little honesty please)

_____
_____
_____
_____
_____

What else are you doing that makes it more difficult?

_____

_____

_____

_____

_____

Some Practical Simple Advice: Stop doing things that hurt the relationship

Beginnings right now, stop doing anything that might be making your relationship worse. Do not try to fix your partner. Do not suggest what they should being doing for you. Do not put pressure on your partner to change. Do not tell your partner all the things they are doing wrong. Leave the conflicts alone for now.

In order for things to change, you are the one who has to change. Yes, even if you are already perfect, there are some things that you can do to shift the dynamics with your partner. But only if you want this relationship to thrive. (I know, someone's got to do it. You can.)

Take one hundred percent responsibility for your relationship. Not fifty percent. Take one hundred percent responsibility for making the relationship work. You must be willing to take your commitment level higher.

I will say that again. You must be willing to take your commitment level higher. You must be willing to do the things you are about to learn here and then implement them immediately. If you do, things are likely to change so fast it will surprise you. It happens all the time for my clients. Now it's your turn.

Reality Check Summary

1. **Tell yourself the truth whatever that is.**
2. **Decide you want a great relationship.**
3. **Make a real commitment.**
4. **Know what you are willing to do about it.**
5. **The facts and numbers have nothing to do with you, but they are very real.**
6. **Stop doing anything that makes the relationship worse, including fixing your partner, pressuring them to change, telling them what they should be doing, etc . . .**
7. **Take one hundred percent responsibility for your relationship.**

#2 BREAKTHROUGH

Check Your Vision

What you fail to consider about the future of your relationship might be just the thing that causes it to fail.

Check Your Vision

After the first five years with my wife, I began to think about the future of our relationship. I started considering the possibility that another level of success existed for me in terms of closeness, connection, and shared passion for each other. Was it possible?

People say that marriage happiness peaks in the first few years, and then everything starts to decline. I didn't believe that to be true, so I began to think of my marriage like most other things in my life . . . as a work in progress; something that I was creating.

How did I want it to ultimately be? I began to ask myself, *what was the most amazing relationship I could imagine, and what would that look like?*

We all get to decide what standard is acceptable in our lives. I wanted to have something extraordinary with my wife so I began to work towards making it happen.

Some people say that everything in life seems to be either growing or dying. Nothing ever remains the same. A relationship is no different than anything else, in that regard. Your relationship is either growing in love or losing love. The connection is either deepening over time, or it's beginning to sever. Your passion for each other is elevating or it's evaporating.

It wasn't enough for me to coast on how well things were going and to imagine that the relationship was on auto pilot. The relationship wasn't going to just magically take care of itself and everything would be perfectly fine. Business doesn't work that way. If you don't work to grow a business, it will naturally decline, and ultimately, fail. If you don't weed your garden, the weeds will take over, eventually. If you don't maintain your car and home they will fall apart.

Effort is required in order to sustain anything at a constant level. Relationships are no different.

Even if I wanted to keep my marriage at a consistent level of *really good*, that meant I'd better do something about it all the time. On its own merits it would tend to decline naturally without a conscious effort to make it better. If I wasn't doing something intentionally to make it great, I was actually neglecting the relationship, and I would suffer the consequences of that neglect.

That was an eye opening realization for me. The consequences of what I call *benign neglect* are what I see in most couples today.

This *benign neglect* is another form of taking each other, and the relationship, for granted. You don't intend to have the connection between you and your partner drift slowly apart, but that's what happens without any real effort to do something about it. No one intends to lose passion for their partner, but that's the result when people expect to just live happily ever after. Are you preoccupied with your busy life putting your partner and the relationship someplace at the bottom of your *to do list*?

The neglect is not intentional, it simply happens because we don't know any better.

If your relationship is important to you, this understanding is essential to your ultimate happiness and success. Either do something every day, which by the way might take as little as two minutes, or risk the consequences of that neglect.

Why did you really get married? What's the real reason . . . what's the truth?

_____
_____
_____
_____
_____

Some people find that they are in an intimate relationship for the wrong reasons. It's not unusual to know people who prefer being with anyone, rather than being alone. Certainly, you have known someone who would rather be with anyone instead of being alone.

If you are in a relationship only to get love, you will be highly disappointed. If you are in a relationship just to have children, it is unlikely to serve either partner or the children. If you are in a relationship because you want to be financially taken care of, you will never be truly happy. If you are in a relationship because all of your friends are in one, you will suffer.

CHECK YOUR VISION

How important is love in your life? How important is it to share your life with a partner in a committed, deeply passionate relationship? How important is it to feel the deliciousness of being intimately connected to someone who is more than just your best friend?

We all get to live our lives the way that we choose based on the decisions that we make. We decide what's acceptable to us in love. We decide what type of partner that we bring into our lives and hold onto or not. We unknowingly choose day by day; to sustain the relationship, to elevate the relationship, or to offer it benign neglect. Which have you been choosing?

_____

_____

Here are few more questions to continue the process . . . .

When you think about your relationship, what are you getting from it? How does it make you feel?

_____

_____

_____

_____

_____

What are you personally contributing to your relationship? How are you making your partner feel?

_____

_____

_____

_____

_____

Do you really know what you want from your relationship? Do you want your partner to mostly leave you alone as some people do? They claim that they have the relationship exactly as they want it . . . both partners doing their own thing and avoiding each other in order to avoid conflict.

What do you want your relationship to look like two years from today? Do you want it to be the same as it is now, or better? How do you want your relationship to be five years from now? How about fifteen years from right now? Imagine your relationship in fifteen years if nothing changes.

If you aren't doing something about your future right now, you are making a big mistake. This is more than something to think about. It's something to *do* something about or not. It's also just another choice to be made.

Can you imagine your relationship in two years time if nothing improves? Will it survive, or separate? You get to decide how your interaction with your partner will be. You get to decide how you want your love life to feel.

One of the biggest mistakes that I see couples make is that they have no vision for their day to day interaction with each other. There is no vision for how they want to be and feel with each other. No thought has gone into how they want to share their lives over time.

Couples certainly haven't thought about what they want their relationship to ultimately look and feel like and what that might mean for how they treat each other right now.

We are all limited by the visions that we create or fail to create for our lives.

Most people just go day by day. They may plan for a house, children, or even retirement, but there is no planning for the emotional aspects of love, passion, deep connection, sharing, communication and intimacy. No thoughts about how they ideally want those things to be. No goal, no target, and no vision in the areas that help the relationship thrive. No ideas about how to sustain lasting love and connection.

What this practically means is that most couples aren't actually working together towards anything in particular. So the emotional aspects that once captivated the couple in the beginning often drifts silently away. That once deep connection gradually diminishes over time. People love each other, but find that they aren't in love any more. The sexual chemistry that was so hot at the start of the relationship barely registers on the thermometer after awhile. People find that they have less and less in common. People often wonder who their partner really is. They begin to take each other for granted. It gets worse.

If there's no bull's eye in the marriage target to aim for, where do people end up? Most relationships that survive are fairly lifeless. In fact, most people not only have no target, they also have nothing truly meaningful that they are aiming for in life with one another. So, they drift apart. It seems perfectly normal because that's what everyone says happens, but it's really a story of low standards and no vision.

The big question is; can people find a path back to deeply re-connecting with each other by themselves without any understanding of how to do it? The chances of that happening are slim to none. You get to decide what you are willing to do to address your own situation and how important that is or isn't to you.

Create a vision in your relationship.

What do you want your interaction with your significant other to be like? How do you want to feel around them? This is especially important in a marriage. If you don't have a vision of where you want this relationship to ultimately be, you will meander through life together going from thing to thing, busy schedules, busy routines, hectic paced lives, pre-occupied with the unimportant or urgent thing of the moment. You will likely take each other for granted. You will treat each other with *benign neglect*. Unaware of what the other needs most from you. You will settle into a quick sand of mediocrity that sucks the life out of both of you. You will feel empty and unfulfilled.

Without a vision, you and your partner can't be the priorities for each other. Without a vision the passionate aliveness of your marriage will pass you by. If you aren't focused on what you really want your relationship to feel like and be like, everything and anything else will always come first.

What are some of the things that come between you and your partner today? Is it work, or other family members, children, crazy out of control routines, or social media, etc? There are so many things that can occupy your mind and time, what's left for your partner?

List a few things that get in the way of your relationship with your significant other:

_____
_____
_____
_____
_____

Roger and Beth

Get some clarity. Roger and Beth became clients after failed couples counseling. They wanted to make a last ditch effort to see if they could save their marriage. When I asked each of them what they wanted the relationship to look like, they each struggled to talk about anything meaningful.

They talked mostly about what they didn't want. They didn't want to fight. They didn't want to avoid each other in order to escape an argument. They didn't like feeling resentful towards each one another. They didn't want to feel the overwhelming stress that was spilling over into their busy careers. They didn't want to feel anxiety when they came home wondering what type of mood the other was in. And most of all, they didn't want to live any longer as they were now.

They also didn't want to end of up like most of their friends. Many of their friends were divorced or separated, and both were thinking that this would be inevitable for them as well.

While it's good to know what you don't want, this isn't a vision. It's not even close. Even if Roger and Beth were to avoid all of those stressful things, where were they headed with each other? If they weren't headed someplace specific, they would end up *no-where.* No passion, no connection, no hope, no aliveness, no communication, and eventually, no love.

I asked them to imagine that they were about to sail on a boat into the Atlantic Ocean, but they didn't know where they wanted to go. Let's say they wanted to be someplace warm. Even if they knew how to avoid the rocks and other ships, if they didn't have a specific destination they would be swept along with the wind and currents, and might end up beached in Haiti, or drift all the way to Antarctica or caught up in the gulf stream of life and carried to Greenland, when they could have easily sailed to The Caymans, or Bermuda, or The Virgin Islands. Which would you prefer?

Take a moment now and write a few things down. What do you want your relationship with your partner to look like? How do you want your personal interaction to be?

How do you want to communicate? What do you want your intimacy to be like? Write down all the aspects of your relationship that matter.

_____
_____
_____
_____
_____
_____
_____
_____
_____
_____

What do you want your relationship to look like five years from now? How do you want to feel with your partner? What's really important to you?

_____
_____
_____
_____
_____
_____
_____
_____
_____
_____

CHECK YOUR VISION

Why not take things up a notch . . . What's the limit between two people who truly love each other?

Dream a little. If you were to create a fantasy marriage for yourself, what would it look like? What does the ultimate ideal marriage look like? If there were no limits to your relationship how would you want it to be? Imagine your ideal romantic fantasy marriage and write the specifics of it here:

_____
_____
_____
_____
_____
_____
_____
_____
_____
_____

No one can tell you what's possible for your relationship. No one can predict how close, or deeply connected, or passionate or loving a marriage can become. It is possible to expand your vision of every aspect of your relationship and make it real. Many of us have, and so can you.

Get Specific. I asked Roger and Beth to make a list of the things that were really important to them in the relationship. This is the beginning of a vision. Here's part of their actual initial list:

Beth—She wanted to feel safe to express herself, feel his support, feel accepted for who she is, have a softer, deeper connection.

Roger—He wanted to laugh more, feel closer to her, have more fun, play more often, have more sex.

I helped them to get even more specific. I asked Beth how she would know if she had Roger's support and what that would look like to her. What would he have to do specifically for her so that she will feel supported? She mentioned a few things right away including; *listening to her closely, paying attention to her when she needed him, feeling that she came first, and valuing her opinion about things while not belittling her ideas.* We continued to identify the specifics that fulfilled her needs. Now there's no guessing game. He knows exactly what she needs and how she needs it. Now it was up to him to commit to doing some of those things.

I asked Roger what would have to happen for him to feel closer to Beth? What exactly did he mean by more fun, more play and more sex? How much more? Was it even about a specific number of times? How would that actually happen for him to be happier? As he talked about his idea of what that meant, what he really wanted was more spontaneity in the relationship. This was a very different need to pursue than simply looking for more fun or more sex.

In order for a relationship to have more spontaneity, someone has to lead. Who was going to lead the fun, play and sex? Roger had wanted Beth to initiate sex more often, but it never happened. It was time for Roger to step up.

Roger made a decision that he would initiate and set the tone for everything that he wanted to have happen in the relationship. By doing this, he was stepping into his masculine role and you could see the genuine impact it was having on her. She agreed to follow his lead and was excited about him being the initiator of things that she would also happily benefit from.

This process doesn't have to be complicated. It can be simple as long as you are very clear about what you want. For example: Imagine that you want to have long-term passion for your partner. Maybe you want to maintain the *off the charts chemistry* that you have with each other today. That's specific enough. You know exactly what passion looks and feels like. Now how do you make that happen?

Here are a few easy suggestions: Hug, kiss, and touch each other often. Talk with your partner about how attracted you are to them. Remind them of the specific things you find sexy about them. Communicate as if you truly love each other, and absolutely no disrespectful name calling. Take care of your appearance and physical body for you and for your partner. Surprise them with an unexpected whisper about what you want to do with them. Allow that thought to sink in for awhile before you act on it. Create a routine of doing something different and exploring sensually. You get the idea. If you do those things regularly, there's no reason for the chemistry between you to diminish, it's more likely to grow and expand. Speaking of chemistry, the next chapter is all about it.

Making the Vision Real. Now that you know what's really important to you, it's time to make it happen by doing something about it every day. You can think of your interaction with your partner like any other goal that you want in your life and aim for it daily by what you do. Your simple actions matter. This will keep you out of the little distractions that tend to stack up over time. It's usually the little things that tend to cause the biggest blow up arguments. Have you had a big disagreement and forgotten what you argued about a week later?

Rachel and Jacob

Rachel didn't like how Jacob drove the car and would constantly be cringing when he got too close to the car in front of him. She would physically put her hands over her face and pull her knees up as if they were about to hit something. Even though she was always perfectly safe, she acted as if she was about to be in an accident at any moment. You can imagine what Jacob thought about this. It was driving him crazy and he had had enough of it.

This little issue (or was it?) was driving a wedge between them. It was causing tremendous stress. Most of the time in order to pacify her, he suggested she drive so he didn't have to listen to it. Sometimes they took two cars. But that wasn't a real solution and he was beginning to resent her. She didn't like what was happening between them and blamed his driving and much more.

When I dug into the issue a little, it was very clear that she didn't trust him, and this lack of trust manifested itself as a driving issue. However, the real trust issue went back a number of years and had been the trigger event that caused the challenge in the relationship.

What Jacob really wanted was passion for each other like they used to have. As you might guess, without trust, true passion doesn't exist and not much was going on in the relationship sexually. It's difficult to want to make love with someone you don't trust.

I asked Jacob to treat Rachel as if she was under his tender loving care as the source for certainty and predictability in her life. That meant paying attention to what she needed in any moment. It also meant he had to get curious about her and what she might really need instead of ignoring her because he couldn't figure it out.

His willingness to provide her with something rock solid rebuilt her trust surprisingly quickly. Things improved in every aspect of the relationship. At one point, he invited her with genuine concern to sit in the back seat because *it was so much safer there*. She declined the offer and the driving gradually became a non issue.

Imagine if someone is under your tender loving care, what might you be willing to do for them in a very real, heartfelt way?

I remember a difficult argument that my wife and I had a number of years back. I have no idea what it was all about, but I remember a moment of total clarity. She said something and I responded unpleasantly, I'm sure. She got angry and said something back. I got angrier and said something else, and then she got more upset at what I had just said. The argument escalated as arguments tend to do.

In a flash of insight it occurred to me that our relationship was in trouble, and if I didn't do something fast, we were going to go down a path that there might be no recovery from. So in an instant I remembered why I was with her, and how much I loved her, and how much I truly wanted her in my life. I changed my tone immediately and said softly, "I am really sorry, you're right and I love you so much."

Now, for her to hear that after an escalation is a bit unexpected. It caught her completely by surprise. She wasn't sure I meant it and said something back almost in a normal tone. Again I said softly, "I really love you, and I am so sorry because I don't want to argue with you at all." She, of course, softened her tone considerably and said that she is sorry too and didn't want to argue either. Result-Disaster avoided. That was easy . . . or absolutely impossible . . . depending on whether you have a vision and the ability to remember what's really important.

By remembering what I really wanted, even though I was distracted for a moment, I was able to shift what might have been a relationship ending situation. I had remembered what was most important to me in that moment of argument . . . and maybe it had saved us. I have never forgotten that clarity.

I want you to remember what's really important to you in the difficult moments that come. They don't go away completely; they just become less and less difficult. Life will continue to throw things at us. We all get stressed from time to time and that's not going to go away. We all face challenges. What we remember to focus on in those moments can make the difference between happiness and heartache.

Your vision for the relationship is that difference.

Vision Summary

1. **Your relationship is either growing in love or losing love.**
2. **Know why you are in a relationship to begin with.**
3. **Know what you are giving to it and getting from it.**
4. **Know what you want your relationship to look like and feel like.**
5. **What's your fantasy marriage look like?**
6. **Get clear and specific about what's really important to you.**

7. Focus and act on your vision every day.
8. In any conflict or struggle remember always what's most important . . . why you are in a relationship with this person and your vision for it.

BREAKTHROUGH #3

Correct the Polarity

The magnetic attraction of sexual chemistry allows the relationship to bloom with aliveness. Your desire for each other is the magic that mutes most challenges.

Correct the Polarity

Sexual chemistry is that incredible sensual feeling that is created when two people are truly attracted to each other. Lots of words like butterflies . . . tingling . . . sparks . . . heat . . . and melting etc . . . have been used to describe the sensations, but none really do it justice. You have definitely felt it and know what I mean. The impact goes far beyond our intellectual understanding. This can feel like an irresistible force within us that we aren't consciously controlling that compels us to desire the other person.

The chemistry of sexual attraction happens to us, and is really not of our own choosing. It just happens. We recognize it immediately when it's there, and we also know right away when we feel nothing for another person. Have you ever been with someone who was really nice and you really liked them, and maybe they were pretty or handsome, but you felt nothing . . . zero chemistry?

This magical chemistry can also be called the spark of polarity, which simply means the attraction of opposites. It is the attraction of opposites that creates the sparks. The opposing energies of masculine and feminine can turn a normal connection into feelings of volcanic sexual attraction for both people.

Do you remember a time when molten sexual sparks flew when you were with that certain someone? Maybe your whole body felt alive. This is polarity, the magnetic pull between two people. It's the key to connection, passion and intimacy. This attracting force of masculine and feminine sexual energy stokes the fires of passion and it sustains passion.

This is similar to the pulling force of energy that attracts between two magnets. However, as you know, if you turn one of the magnets around, thus shifting the magnetic poles, they will then repel each other. This is what happens in relationships. Reverse the polarity of just one partner and the spark of attraction is gone. That means if you change the chemistry or mix of masculine and female energy balance in a relationship then the attraction disappears.

The specific mix of chemistry that exists between two people; one with masculine energy and one with feminine energy is essential to sustaining long term sexual attraction. It keeps things hot.

Do you love them, but aren't in love with them? *Blame Polarity.* Your initial attracting mix of masculine and feminine energy balance has shifted. Are you less physically attracted to your partner? *Blame Polarity.* Usually, one or both partners are acting with a different mix of masculine or feminine energy and it's wreaking havoc on the magnetic chemistry.

Is your sex life dull or non—existent? *Blame Polarity.* Now, the magnetic energy mix has shifted even more so that there's barely an attraction. Are conflicts increasing in your relationship? *Blame Polarity.* When the polarity energy is different, couples find it more difficult to communicate with each other.

Have you ever been in a relationship where you were initially totally attracted to your partner, and over time, you just lost that sense of attraction and connection? Maybe it was even hard to recognize at the time, but somehow you lost your interest in them physically. Even if it was incredibly passionate early on in the relationship, something shifted. Can you remember a specific time?

That happens when polarity gets reversed and those magnetic poles begin to repel each other. Someone in the relationship or both partners have shifted their energies just enough to create an opposing reaction. Maybe the man became less masculine and a woman became less feminine in moments that mattered, and over time it caused the polarity to reverse, just like turning the magnets.

The polarity of masculine and feminine energy is essential to every successful relationship including gay and lesbian relationships. Everyone has, and uses both masculine and feminine energy, but what matters is which specific mix predominated for you that attracted your partner and how you sustain that in the relationship.

What was the combination of masculine and feminine balance that existed at the beginning of your relationship that caused that deep, special, sexual attraction? Is it different now? How has it changed?

_____
_____
_____
_____
_____
_____

Here are a few simple characteristics of masculine and feminine energy:

Masculine energy—focused, stands strong, decisive, direct and protective. Masculine wants to experience freedom.

Feminine energy—open, free flowing, nurturing, indirect, and intuitive. Feminine wants to experience love.

Let's go for a little journey back in time . . .

Do you remember a time when you were totally attracted to someone? Can you remember a specific time when you just felt that intense connection? Maybe there was just something special about that person, and maybe you didn't even know why, but the feeling of it was so amazing. It could have started with a look, or something they said, or the way they smiled and melted you, or the way they moved, or when they got really close to you and leaned in . . . remember that . . . and then, the attraction just started growing, expanding, . . . deeper, even brighter. That's right . . . feeling that deep connection. You can easily imagine it fully.

Now, feel those feelings of that intense connection as if you were there . . . with them right now . . . experiencing it as if it was happening again. How were you breathing? Breathe that way now. What were you seeing? See it even bigger . . . and brighter. How were you feeling? Feel that even more profoundly now. What were you hearing? Hear that in stereo as you imagine being there again . . .

Maybe you had this deep desire to . . . touch them, . . . kiss them . . . hold them . . . make love with them. The magnetic pull of sexual attraction was working its' magic on you, . . . and you were so drawn in that maybe time seemed to stop as you imagine the total aliveness of that deeply sensual feeling. Drinking all of the sweetness of it again . . .

Even if it's been a while, you can remember it now can't you?

That's the magnetic pull of polarity . . . when the sparks fly between two people . . . it's unmistakably hot. Sometimes, it's unforgettable. It can be the beginning of something incredible, or the beginning of pain.

That spark of sexual chemistry is what pulls people together and, like any spark, it can become an intense inferno that takes on a life of its' own, or it can completely lose its' moment and burn out slowly. Sometimes the fire gets the life snuffed out of it seemingly out of nowhere.

How important is polarity? Lack of polarity is number one cause of divorce between married couples in my opinion. It's the creator of that sense of aliveness that exists in every deeply connected, successful, loving, intimate relationship. If you want to feel that deep sense of connection with your partner, there must be polarity. If you want to have long term sexual chemistry, there must be polarity.

If you don't want passion, or deep connection, then don't worry about it because every lifeless relationship lacks polarity. This lack of polarity is the silent killer of marriages and long term relationships. Maybe you know of some couples in lifeless relationships where no intimacy exists. The relationship has become at best a friendship. For some people that's enough. It's simply a standard of what they are willing to accept in their lives. You get to decide what's acceptable for you too . . . remember?

Here's an example: Attraction can occur between a feminine woman and a masculine man; or a feminine man and a masculine woman. Both can work equally well. (There are many shades and subtleties of this energy, and it's simply important to remember that you need both to create attraction.) However, bring together a masculine man and a masculine woman and there will be no attraction. Put together a feminine man and a feminine woman and you get no magnetic attraction. These couples might easily be great friends, but a disaster for any long term romantic involvement.

How do you sustain this special mix of polarity that feels so extraordinary?

Most couples find that the spark of sexual attraction diminishes over time even though it doesn't have to be that way. They lose that special feeling of chemistry that they intially had for each other. Passion, intimacy, sexuality, and feeling deeply connected with someone are highly important needs that must exist for the relationship to be successful and different than any friendship. As I mentioned and it's worth repeating again, this is the top cause of divorce in my opinion.

It takes a masculine spark and a feminine spark to create fireworks in any relationship. We are conditioned to believe that the feelings gradually subside. After fourteen years with my wife, the heat of our chemistry is still burning strong. I know other couples who have been together for much longer who enjoy that same special bond with each other. You can too.

You can re-ignite the sexual passion in your relationship by restoring the polarity. Here's an example:

Linda and Reggie

Linda and Reggie had an incredible connection; they knew something was unusual about the intensity of their chemistry from the moment that they were introduced.

Reggie's story:

"There was just something so sexy about Linda. She had this killer body and this smile, and I couldn't keep my hands off of her. We had sex all the time . . . Everywhere . . . Wild sex. Today there's nothing. Zero. I have no interest in her sexually. We argue all the time. She gets defensive every time I say something. We haven't had sex in well over a year."

Linda's story

"Reggie was so hot. He had those piercing eyes that made me feel tingly inside. He had this confidence about him that was irresistible. We made love a lot in the beginning, I felt like he really listened to everything I said. He gave me

tons of attention and I loved to kiss him. Then something just died, it didn't seem like we connected anymore. He seemed distant. I began to not trust him."

Looking at Polarity

In the beginning of the relationship, Reggie was very confident and strong. He made lots of decisions about what they would do for dinner or entertainment. He listened closely to Linda's challenges with her family and work. He initiated sex. All of this is masculine energy.

Then Reggie had a problem at his company. There were lots of layoffs and he began to stress out about whether he would be next on the chopping block. Even as a senior manager, there was no job security. He was having trouble communicating with Linda. She always wanted to know what he was going to do about his job uncertainty. Her questions were stressing him out more and more.

He began to lose his confidence and feel uncertain about their future together. He had begun to lose his masculine energy in the relationship. He argued with her about how she could also initiate sex from time to time. He went through half hearted motions of listening to her talk about the non-stop details of her family situation. He told her what he thought she should do, and became frustrated because she never did it. He began to come up with ways to avoid her anger and emotional outbursts.

The polarity had shifted. Reggie was no longer carrying the same masculine energy that initiated the sparks in the relationship. He had unknowingly adopted some traits that were feminine in style.

Linda had let Reggie make most of the decisions at the beginning of the relationship, and now she was making all of the household decisions including the financial decisions. She blamed Reggie for spending too much money on things that they didn't need. She was making all of the decisions about the children and was directing the social schedule for the family and organizing school activities. Linda and Reggie argued about the discipline of the children. She felt like she was alone and became more protective of herself. Linda had lost some of her feminine essence and began to take on more masculine energy.

She began to direct Reggie when he came home, telling him all the things that needed to be done around the house that he was neglecting. She was angry with him that he was never available when she needed him. She nagged at him about spending more time with the kids. She criticized him often. The job uncertainty was getting to her and she demanded that he have a conversation with his boss, while reminding him that he was spending too much money. Even if she was right, none of this was helpful to the relationship.

Reggie began to spend more time at work and she started to wonder if he might actually be having an affair because he didn't return her calls or texts right away. She began to not trust him and accused him of being someplace else. When he did come home, all he did was get on the computer or in front of the TV. She had so much to do and he wasn't helping at all. She began to resent him. She couldn't get his attention about things that she wanted to talk about, so she started spending more and more time talking with her girl friends. Linda had shifted her polarity to more of a masculine essence. The attraction was no longer there.

Some Quick Solutions

Reggie needed to step up his masculine presence if he wanted to restore trust. That meant giving Linda his full attention when she spoke with him, actually, more than just his attention . . . to give his entire focus. Women know when they talk to men whether they are engaged with them or distracted. They can feel it. Have you ever tried to talk to man in the middle of a big sports playoff game, or something really important for his work? You know you won't have his total attention. This is what happens often in our fast paced, hectic, stressed out lives. Our attention spans are shorter and shorter and lead to severing connections between men and women.

I guided Reggie to look deeply into Linda's eyes to see if he could feel what she was feeling. To explore what was happening deep inside her emotionally and see if he might be able to figure out what really was going on. By stepping into this masculine presence, the very thing that she was missing, things could change quickly if he did it reasonably well.

For the feminine, feeling a masculine presence is extremely reassuring. There's a feeling of safety and comfort that exists in those moments when the man's total presence and attention are given. The feminine feels connected, listened to, heard, and possibly (yes this is a stretch sometimes) even understood.

When this presence is practiced, the masculine can gain insight into what the feminine needs the most in that moment. That's when she feels that he "*gets me*." Almost as if he can read her mind he is so in touch with what she needs from him.

Words are often best kept to a minimum. The feminine simply needs to be heard. The appropriate *"I'm sorry,"* or *"I am here for you,"* or *"you're right"* will come in handy. The tone of voice while in this moment of heartfelt presence has enormous potential to create a moment of deep connection, even when one has been missing for years.

I also recommended that Reggie make no suggestions about what Linda should do about her family situation unless she asked him specifically for his thoughts about it, and even then to be careful. No feminine wants to be fixed by the masculine. No one enjoys being criticized. The only fixing that the masculine should be doing is things around the house.

Linda was asked to have heartfelt understanding for what Reggie was going through. She was so caught up in her head that she lost touch with her feminine heart. I asked her to put aside her past hurts for a moment, and show him that she still loved him and believed in him.

She began to recognize that sometimes he needed to kick back and chill out because that's how men rebuild testosterone and restore the masculine balance. Men shift their brain activity down at night and like to do mindless things, like watch TV, read, surf the net, work on a hobby, etc. She made some space for Reggie to make some household decisions for the family again which also helped restore some masculine balance. It was hard for her to give up that control because it had made her feel like she had an important role in the family besides being a mom.

Linda also needed to replenish some of her feminine energy. Feminine energy is restored when women care for themselves first by filling themselves up with things that make them feel good. That way, they have more to give to others. That might come in the form of self pampering; massage, manicures, girls nights out, shopping, working out, wearing feminine colors, taking scented baths, or sexy clothing, etc. These are also ways of restoring oxytocin, otherwise known as the love hormone. This is the chemical of deep connection and attachment that women need to replenish.

Women will often tend to their own needs last and tell me, *"Who has time for any of that"*. I often reply with, *"Ok, how's not doing that working for you so far? Are you happy? How do you feel about you?"* There are so many choice points in life. You can choose to nurture yourself or choose the consequences of not doing it. Happiness, like many things in life is a choice.

Scientifically, it's known that the fastest way to deplete testosterone and oxytocin is from stress, and the fast pace of our lives creates lots of that. The more we can relax and take time for our own self care, the more we build and replenish our stores of the chemicals that create attraction and replenish our natural energy. Take some time for you. You're worth it.

Results

Both Linda and Reggie were pleasantly surprised at how quickly they noticed subtle changes in each other. Reggie said that Linda had softened considerably in the first week. She appeared more attractive to him. Their conversations had become much less stressful, and they had hugged and cuddled a number of times.

Linda said that she felt Reggie's presence for the first time in years. It reminded her of all the reasons why she was attracted to him in the beginning. She thought she would have a really tough time letting go of past hurts, but when he showed up for her as the focused, attentive fully present man, she felt safe. She expressed her surprise at how she was beginning to feel that maybe she could open up to him. She wasn't ready to trust him fully, but there was a definite renewal in the relationship. This change took just over a week.

The couple continued to progress through my 90 Day Relationship Challenge and rediscovered the love and intimate passion that had been missing for so many years. Now they have a solid foundation of connection and the tools and skills to make their relationship anything that they want it to be.

Time to put your polarity back in place:

For Men and Women; Were you more *masculine* (decisive, strong, protective, direct in communication style) or more *feminine* (open, indirect communication, more heart feeling, intuition, nurturing, free flowing) at the beginning of the relationship when the attraction was the highest?

How has your masculine/feminine energy shifted over the course of your relationship? What's different about it now?

_____
_____
_____
_____
_____

What can you do to restore the masculine/feminine balance within you? What do you need to do for you?

_____
_____
_____
_____
_____

***Personal note to men—some of these strategies that you will read might seem counter intuitive. Do them anyway, because they work. I had a tough time wrapping my head around some of what I was discovering and learning, and initially I was resistant. But, I decided to continue to test the ideas and experiment for myself. Not only did they work, they worked every time without fail and they worked fast. I have made them a constant practice in my life and client work.

Understanding how to restore Polarity is perhaps the most essential skill to have in order to rekindle the flames of passion and to restore love and connection. It can work magic in your relationship. It won't happen by itself, someone has to do something if you want things to change. Will that be you, or will you settle for a lifeless, passionless marriage like so many others?

Summary

1. **Sexual Chemistry is the spark of attraction also known as Polarity**
2. **Polarity is the attraction of opposites. Masculine/Feminine are opposite energies.**
3. **Everyone has masculine and feminine energy that is available to them.**

4. The correct mix of your masculine/feminine balance is crucial in restoring polarity in your relationship.
5. Understand the Differences between Masculine and Feminine energy.
6. Polarity gets reversed unknowingly because of life and relationship stressors. It can happen quickly, or slowly over time.
7. Take care of yourself first to correct your masculine/feminine energy imbalances.
8. There are things you can do right now to correct the imbalance of polarity and restore the passion and connection in your relationship.

#4 BREAKTHROUGH

A2—Attention and Appreciation

It's the little things that we fail to do that devastate the relationship drip by poisonous drip. Benign neglect is everywhere.

A2—Attention and Appreciation

By far, the biggest complaint that I hear from men is that their spouses don't show them enough appreciation. I hear it constantly. They feel unappreciated for all the things that they do to provide for the family, the sacrifices they make, the life styles they provide and it all seems to be expected without so much as a thank you. These men often feel an undercurrent of resentment for being taken for granted, or bitter because they feel like they are being taken advantage of. This happens even when both partners work full time.

When I bring this up with the spouse, or partner, they assure me that they are appreciating their man all the time. This simply isn't true, because whatever they think they are doing is not working. They may be recognizing him in ways that don't translate well to the masculine. They may be offering appreciation that might be subtly implied instead of stated outright. Mostly though, it's simply not there.

I hear this complaint whether the wife has a professional career or not. I hear it if the woman is the main source of income for the family. It goes deep. This lack of appreciation grinds men down over time. It wears on their desire to want to understand their partner. It erodes their willingness to want to work on the relationship. It can evolve into a low level anger that gets described as *"I'm done,"*, meaning they've had enough and can't be bothered to exert any more effort to work on the relationship. They don't care anymore.

Women, of course, also want and need to be appreciated. Based on my experience there's another aspect of appreciation that they need even more. This presents itself in the form of attention, and women need their man's attention frequently. Attention provides the woman a solid foundation of certainty and comfort; it also contributes to feelings of connectedness, and reassurance. All things the feminine craves.

A2—ATTENTION AND APPRECIATION

When a man gives a woman his full attention she feels like she is highly valued to him and more deeply connected in that moment. Without a man's focused attention, trust can begin to erode quickly. Where trust goes, respect often follows. You can easily imagine how closed a woman is to a man she doesn't trust and respect. There can be no sexual attraction. That's why relationships without trust and respect have little or no intimacy. If it happens at all, it's out of a sense of guilt or obligation and she feels disgusted for even doing it.

Without a man's presence of attention, women interpret that it's no longer safe to share feelings and important details of life. Being heard is really important for the feminine. So she closes herself emotionally to the man when this doesn't happen. This is the exact opposite of the feminine energy that is needed to sustain polarity.

Here's a scenario: Tom and Heather

Tom is on his laptop working on a project for his company and is totally engrossed in an email he is writing to his boss about some financial projections. Heather wants to talk to him about something that's happened at work with her co-worker. She begins to talk and Tom nods un—huh without looking up from his key pad still typing away. She asks if he's listening and he says nothing for a moment. She then says, "Tom did you hear what I said," and he looks up and says "just a minute, I want to finish this email". Sounds innocent enough doesn't it, or does it?

Imagine that this scenario continues with Tom as he's watching TV, or on some social media site, or texting someone or reading. The downside to all this lack of attention is that a new meaning about Tom gets created. If Tom always has something more important to do than listen to anything that Heather has to say, she feels isolated. How can she trust someone who isn't there for her when she needs him? It's easy for Tom to become untrustworthy. She needs him often and it reassures her of the connection. In this scenario, Heather doesn't feel important in Tom's life if he remains unavailable for her. Is any of this resonating with you?

Now let's imagine Tom is ready to listen, and, as Heather starts to share what's going on, Tom interrupts and says, *"Heather, you need to go to your boss and tell him X, Y and Z. This is one of those things that you have to be proactive about. You can't wait. You need to have a conversation with your boss about this. Why don't you start looking for another job If this was me, I wouldn't put up with this. What's wrong with you?"*

Does Heather feel listened to? Of course not! Tom is trying to fix the situation and all Heather wanted was to be heard. This might have been a very minor situation that

A2—ATTENTION AND APPRECIATION

Tom is blowing totally out of proportion with his reaction because maybe he has heard about this problem before. This situation may not even be a big deal to Heather. Maybe she just wanted to connect with Tom and feel his reassuring presence.

Heather might have been stressed out about any number of things and just wanted to talk to and share with her man. Now he wants to fix the situation, and worse, maybe he thinks she needs fixing. This conversation will end badly in an argument, or silent resentment. Take any number of these types of situations and play them out over time and women will stop trusting their partners. It's inevitable.

No woman wants to be fixed by her man. No woman wants her man to fix anything that she talks about unless it has something to do with the house or car, or if she asks him specifically for his insight and even then, she might not really want it. Tread very cautiously here men. Women want no part of our fixing.

When men try to fix things that women want to talk about, it sets up an immediate defensiveness in the female. *"This man doesn't understand me, or what I need, and is completely unavailable for me. I certainly don't need him or any of his fixing"* is a common feminine complaint.

The next time she approaches Tom, she will be more cautious. Soon, she won't even bother to talk to him about her challenges, or stressors, or things that are bothering her because he will get frustrated and try to fix it. She can't trust him to just listen intently to what she's saying, and be supportive of her. When the lack of trust gets bigger, respect begins that slow circle down the toilet with it. Passion, . . . intimacy, . . . connection? Forget it, unless this cycle changes.

Now, Tom has two thoughts going on in his head as Heather talks, *what's her point* and *can I fix it.* The feminine conversation is often loaded with details and information that flows in and out of the man's normal attention span. He wants her to get to the point as quickly as possible so he can give her his solution. He's eager to make her happy and solve any problems. He's wired to be solution oriented and fix things. It makes him feel significant to be able to be there for her.

Unfortunately this will not create any love or connection, nor any passion and heartfelt understanding. It will create a rift between masculine Tom and feminine Heather that can get as wide as the Grand Canyon and seem impossible to piece back together.

This is the one of the core causes of miscommunication between men and women. Men are always looking for

A2—ATTENTION AND APPRECIATION

a main point and needing to fix something. Women are simply looking for a safe place to be heard and to feel connected. In the presence of a man who is giving his full attention a woman feels that she can open up to this man safely. And to her that feels amazing. It's reassuring to her that everything, including the relationship is ok.

Men want more than anything to make their woman happy. If you're a woman reading this, you may have doubts about that from your personal experience. The reality is, if a man feels that no matter what he does, he can't make his woman happy, the tendency is for the man to give up. For him, the relationship becomes a dead end and offers him no satisfaction.

Here's an example of how deep this runs in the man. Around the world men consistently answer this question the same way: How do you feel when you can't make your woman happy? Answers: *Bad, terrible, awful, or like shit!* That translates to *like a failure* for those who don't speak basic man talk.

Heather simply needs Tom to listen and look her in the eyes. To know that she is the center of his universe for those moments makes her feel valued and loved. To know that she is important enough for him to drop what he's doing and pay total attention to her. When he does that, the connection deepens, trust increases, and respect rises.

When a man brings his full presence of attention to the woman it amps of her feminine energy and rekindles the spark of attraction. These connections are felt. They are not intellectual. If you are a woman reading this, you know how great it feels when you get the full presence of a masculine man. Many women describe the feeling of melting blissfully in the full presence of their masculine man.

Another Example: Patrick

Patrick was unhappy with his marriage. He had been married for nineteen years and been *"working his ass off,"* as he described it to me. The fast paced hectic life of an entrepreneur was taking its toll on him. He was feeling depressed and couldn't figure out why. As we got to know each other, and began to figure out how this was specifically affecting his life, it became clear that the source of his problem seemed to be his marriage.

The last three years had been particularly tough on Patrick because of the economy and the normal challenges of any medium sized business. He had lost his decisiveness, and his confidence. He just wasn't feeling like his old self and he didn't know what to do about it.

A2—ATTENTION AND APPRECIATION

At first he didn't want to spend any time talking about his relationship. He felt that work was the cause of this low point in his life. As he finally opened up about his marriage, he revealed an undercurrent of bitterness towards his wife that I often see. His relationship uncertainty had simply spilled over into every other area of his life and had confused him.

In that moment, the source of his problem was clear. When men feel they are in a great relationship, they feel appreciated and valued. This appreciation creates a solid foundation of confidence and decisiveness. Appreciated men are happy men. Again, appreciation also goes a long way for women, it's just slightly different.

Within a few weeks, when Patrick's wife began to thank him and show her genuine appreciation for what he contributed to the family, he brightened up considerably. She found a lot of small ways to catch him doing things right and thank him. Within sixty days, Patrick was feeling like the old confident Patrick, and the marriage improved. Now that Patrick was feeling her gratitude and appreciation there wasn't anything he wouldn't do for his wife.

You may have heard the expression, "it takes two". Sometimes, it takes two people, but one person must be committed. One person must always go first to meet the needs of their partner. People can wait forever for the other person to give first so that then finally they can give back. In that situation, the only outcome is more suffering where they could be joy, more pain where there could be pleasure.

How do you show your partner your appreciation? How often?

_____
_____
_____
_____
_____

What is your honest assessment of your total focused presence and attention for your partner?

_____
_____
_____
_____
_____

What can you do to improve it?

_____
_____
_____
_____
_____

A2—ATTENTION AND APPRECIATION

There is no rule that says to; limit the appreciation that you give to your partner. No place does it say, don't give your partner the attention that they deserve. There is no unwritten rule that says, rarely show your gratitude for what your spouse does for you. Attention and Appreciation are instrumental in the elevation of any relationship and it's in very short supply in most relationships today.

Give your partner more of what they really need. Not what you think they might need. Start with giving more appreciation for you man and more attention and reassurance for your woman. They will notice it right away and typically what you get back will be a pleasant surprise. It doesn't take long to rebuild the connection that once seemed impossible. Get it right and trust can be restored much faster than you might think.

Summary

1. **Men need to feel appreciated in the relationship. There are countless ways to do that.**
2. **Women also need to feel appreciated. It serves her more in the form of attention and even reassurance.**
3. **Women need to feel the total attention of their man, frequently.**
4. **His full presence is required to create trust and respect. Without it they erode quickly.**

5. Long term relationships need trust and respect in order to sustain passion and intimacy.
6. Someone has to commit to making the relationship a priority if it's going to be successful.
7. Give your partner what they really need, not what you think they need.

BREAKTHROUGH #5

Button Pushing Push Back

*If business success is all in your head,
relationship success is found in your heart.*

Button Pushing Push Back

If you've been in your relationship for any reasonable period of time you know that there are times when you don't always agree with your partner. Maybe you've had an argument or two over the years . . . maybe more than two hundred of them.

In any disagreement or misunderstanding, emotions have a tendency to take over. The self protective mechanism kicks in and the fight *to be right* is on. Defending your position becomes what matter most. The reason for the disagreement, or argument is usually not something big. Have you ever been there?

What people do and say in escalating disagreements can be devastating to the relationship. Your partner will push your buttons and get to you from time to time. You will push your partner's buttons unknowingly and upset them. In the heat of the moment, anything is possible.

This ability to get to your partner can become a weapon of choice both consciously and unconsciously in disagreements. People tend to create patterns with each other that can be destructive. It's time to break the patterns that destabilize the relationship.

What would happen if you met this button pushing without resistance? What if you responded back in a way that was light hearted, or loving, or playful and unpredictable, would anything change?

If your partner is upset and lashes out at you, and you say, *"Honey, I love you so much and I am so grateful to have you in my life,"* to whatever tone they use with you, what would happen? Would the argument escalate? Not likely. This one sentence has enough power to completely shift the situation.

It makes sense to evaluate the effectiveness of whatever reactions, responses and patterns of communication that you are caught up in with your partner. Some of them probably need to change if you want your relationship to improve. How well is what you have been doing working for you up to now? If it's not effective, it's time for a new strategy. Of course you do believe in doing only the things that are beneficial to the relationship right?

We all have stressors in our lives that affect our ability to communicate with the empathy and tone that we intend. We get caught up in the moment. These moments get stacked one on top of the other over time, and the tiniest thing can become an enormous blow-out argument.

Most couples have disagreements, which is perfectly ok. Some disagreements remain the entire lives of couples who are in loving, committed marriages. People can agree to simply disagree. People can recognize that there are times when a couple might simply not relate to each other's position on something. In great relationships, the partners let it go because they realize in the bigger picture it's not that important. If they disagree on a few small things it's really not a big deal.

Norma and Curtis

Norma and Curtis seemed to be in endless fights with each other and couldn't seem to avoid them. Curtis would make a comment and Norma would immediately feel that she was being attacked so she would react back with hostility. Norma met with me alone and told me that they intentionally kept their interaction with each other at a minimal level because the stress was too great.

My solution was to get them to lighten up with each other. When Norma came home from work late, Curtis was usually sitting in front of the TV as the kids ran wildly around the house. She would always make a comment about what he wasn't doing. Didn't he see the mess? Didn't he see what the kids were or weren't doing, didn't he have work to do, etc? She walked in anticipating that she would find him in the same spot and the stress began to build before she even walked in the door. This isn't healthy.

She also anticipated walking into a mess that she alone would have to clean up. That *mess* was made up of everything Curtis wasn't doing or was doing wrong. It included everything she normally would have to do, as well as all the extra things she now had to do because of his laziness or lack of interest. You can imagine how much she relished the sight of Curtis.

Because I was only working with Norma, I had no idea about Curtis' perspective on the situation, but it didn't matter. One committed person can work wonders.

I suggested that the next time Norma came home for her to say to Curtis, "Honey I love you so much, thank you for keeping the kids safe". She wasn't happy about my suggestion because she knew he was the problem, and that everything was his fault. But, she decided to try it out just out of curiosity. She thought he would think she was being sarcastic, so I told her how important her tone of voice had to be. We practiced it a bit because it had to have softness and appreciation in it. The tone of her actual genuine gratitude for keeping the kids safe was what was needed. This couldn't be faked. She had to feel it. This had to be real for her if she wanted it to be effective in this situation.

She walked into the room skeptical, but found her words to resonate with the truth, the kids were in fact, safe. Much to her amazement, he was completely speechless and immediately got off the couch to help her with dinner. While he said nothing in response to that comment, she told me that the entire night was completely stress free. They actually enjoyed dinner with the kids together for the first time in what seemed like ages, and he volunteered to get the kids put in bed while she relaxed. This was all new and completely unimaginable to her resulting from this simple, single, heartfelt sentence.

What happened? How could one sentence change things so dramatically?

The reason it worked so effectively was because it broke the pattern that had enveloped the two of them. He was expecting the usual angry Norma to walk in the door and give him a hard time. When she changed her approach to his presence on the couch it would have been very difficult for him to have reacted in his usual way. In my experience, when one person changes their operating style in a normal communication cycle, then the other person must respond differently. This opens the door to a new level of interacting.

You probably realize that we can't control anyone, although we like to try from time to time. We do, however, have the ability to influence people beyond our understanding. We are in fact, influencing people around us all the time, sometimes for the benefit of the relationship and other times not so much.

Imagine what might happen in your relationship if you were to adopt a new strategy for communication. It might be the catalyst for things to change.

Is it possible that you could become more effective in your communication patterns with your partner? How would it feel to know you had that ability to shift the downward spiral of communication in your relationship?

What do you now say that immediately triggers an upset or angry response from your partner? Maybe you even know that saying this will upset them, but from time to time, you do it anyway in the heat of the moment. Write your strategy for non-loving communication.

_____
_____
_____
_____
_____

David

David was on the edge. He had just texted his wife that *the final days are here*. To him, the marriage was over. As a last resort, he decided to work with me to see there was anything he could do to save his marriage. Adding to his dilemma were their three young children. It pained him greatly to imagine someone else raising and influencing them.

David talked with me about his wife's interpretation that most of his communication was angry towards her. He felt helpless because it seemed as if she was constantly complaining about him. Whatever he said, she immediately became defensive and it always ended with an argument. He withheld so much from her just to keep the peace that his own stress levels were bubbling over.

Her chief complaint was that he never spent enough time with the kids and didn't help around the house. Normally, he defended himself because he was working so hard to provide for the family that he struggled to find more time. He was exhausted as it was from all of the stress. Every time he talked about how hard he was working, it caused an increase in hostility from her, and when she was hostile, which was often, she pushed every button on him and he couldn't take much more of it. She also complained constantly about things that he said he would do, but never got around to doing. He figured that divorce was inevitable.

While David had the courage to seek out my input, he admitted that his commitment level wasn't as high as it should be because other than the children, the negativity in their communication had changed the way he viewed his wife. He didn't like who she was when she was angry. He thought he still loved her, but certainly wasn't in love with her anymore. He really wanted clarity around the reality of the situation.

We talked about his choices in very blunt terms. Divorce, separation, or attempts to repair the relationship were all on the table as very real possibilities. As we explored the potential consequences and benefits of each option, it was clear that he wanted to do everything he could to save the marriage for the sake of the children ages seven, nine and twelve. He didn't want to lose his family.

Here's some of my perspective . . .

When people tell me that they are committed, I believe them. They think that they are. Often, they don't understand what that really means. In between consultations with me, there are tasks that I ask everyone to do. Their verbal commitment is much less relevant to me than someone's willingness to do everything that I ask of them.

Some of these tasks aren't easy. Some of them require courage and a willingness to step out of comfort zones. Working with me is not for people who want to make half hearted attempts to change their lives. There's a very clear direct connection between how fast things change, and the percentage of the agreed upon tasks that people actually complete.

I welcome constant feedback based on the tasks that I assign. I want to know for certain how much of what I ask someone to do they are actually doing. Normally,

I have a very good idea of that based on how quickly situations shift, and client feedback allows me to make instant adjustments to tasks if needed. This dynamic learning process is essential to client success. Clients are always aware of their own progress toward what they want because it's continuously measured.

When I work with one person, I have only one perspective of the relationship. There are always two sides to every story, but sometimes I can only work with one partner because of the circumstances. When I work with one person, I hold them one hundred percent responsible for the relationship. It's all up to them, and if they can't own that responsibility for whatever reason, the relationship will fail or remain loveless and lifeless unless the other person magically re-commits on their own.

David's wife was frustrated as evidenced by her anger toward him. Clearly the relationship stress was affecting her. It was also deeply affecting the children. It wasn't a healthy situation for any of them.

My immediate goal was to shift the dynamic within the home in order to reduce stress levels. I talked with David about how he thought his wife was handling things overall. He mentioned that he wasn't sure because she was on the phone with her sister or her girl friends constantly and wasn't paying much attention to him. This was to be expected because if he wasn't meeting her need for connection, she would seek to fulfill that need someplace else.

We talked about the possible emotional impact on her, and her unhappiness. I asked David to imagine having heartfelt understanding for what she was going through. To imagine the stress she must feel as a result of the marriage chaos. This had to be traumatic for her as well.

I asked David to use this heartfelt understanding to soften every one of his reactions to his wife. David had made her feel completely uncertain about the future of their family and she was falling apart before his eyes, but he wasn't able to see it. He was too caught up in his own experience to notice. She was likely devastated by this situation as well.

I suggested that he tap into how she must feel and respond with a heartfelt, "Maybe you're right," or something similar when she criticized or lashed out at him. I suggested he add an "I'm sorry," where appropriate, but only if was real, and only if he wanted the marriage to survive. She would know instantly if it was only words. Many women even know if the man is distracted in the midst of an embrace. They sense these things more than men realize.

I never spoke with David's wife, but I imagined that she viewed him as the person solely responsible for destroying her dream of marriage and family, even though that wasn't true. She also was an active participant in this relationship disaster, but I was only working with him, and would never have a chance to talk about her role in the downfall of the relationship.

In any relationship, two people always participate. As I mentioned, there are always two sides to every story, and often and third possibility. Placing the blame and pointing fingers at only one person means that the other person has zero responsibility in the relationship. To me this is nonsense.

Rarely are there people who are unwilling to give their partner anything at all in a marriage. Most relationships that struggle are not because one person is a giver and the other person only a taker. That situation would be highly unusual even though people often mistakenly perceive it to be that way.

When things are going wrong, it's easy to look for what's wrong and find plenty of evidence to support the "everything is his/her fault" theory. It's much easier than looking inside of ourselves for the responsibility that we have in the co-creation of any relationship train wreck.

It's possible that one partner can become so hurt that they cannot give back. It's possible that one person can be so shut down from their disappointment that they aren't able to ever respond to love from that partner again. These situations do occur from time to time. However, most partners will respond favorably to loving gestures that disrupt patterns of negativity.

David honored his commitment. I asked him not to commit to me because that was irrelevant. The commitment had to be made to himself, because one of the worst things in life is the pain of regret. How long would he regret not doing everything that he could to save his marriage and the family that was so important to him? How long would he regret watching someone else raise and influence his children?

That pain can last a lifetime. David had to be able to look himself in the mirror at the end of the day and know that he had done everything that he could to try to shift the relationship. To know without a doubt that he had truly given this his best effort. That required courage on an ongoing basis and David demonstrated that to me through the variety of things that he did.

When David met his wife's anger the first time with a heartfelt, "*Maybe you're right,*" she stopped in mid sentence and looked at him for a few seconds. He shrugged his shoulders and said *"maybe you're right"* again. She responded without being upset and it created an opening for him to genuinely apologize to her. David told me that he could finally see the pain in her eyes. This was a huge turning point. He finally realized that beneath all of her tough exterior, there was tremendous sadness and hurt.

They talked softly together as he talked with her about his commitment to work things out, and he told me that her eyes filled with tears. They hugged for the first time in many months. It was the beginning of the recovery of his marriage.

He began to give his wife his total attention any time she wanted to speak with him. He gave the children his full attention when he was with them too, but they came after her. The result was that the criticism became less and less every day. The impact on the family and home environment was swift as everyone's stress levels dropped off. Good feelings began to replace the stress. Everything had changed because the marriage was no longer at risk.

All of this was possible because David put his own personal hurt and frustration aside. He had become the leader of his family. He single handedly saved his marriage because he made the commitment and followed through on it. He had put his wife's needs and the needs of the relationship above his own, and she responded to him with love and affection. That's how fast it usually works when one person is absolutely committed. David had delivered one hundred percent on everything that I had asked him to do.

It wasn't always easy. Nothing worthwhile ever is. There were plenty of times David struggled and wondered whether it would work. There were times he thought about what he wasn't getting, but he persisted, and focused on the changes he noticed in her.

The great thing about learning these skills is that you can have them for a lifetime. David not only saved his marriage, he now had the understanding of what he needed to do keep his marriage happy. David's commitment made the difference. How committed are you to shift your relationship?

When people push our buttons, we don't have to push back. We can soften and respond with love, humor, playfulness, or lightness. Even silence can occasionally be helpful.

From time to time in my own marriage I have responded to a tone of upset with playfulness. For example, *"I love it when you're grumpy, it kind of turns me on,"* or *"Did you say you wanted a hug, because I need one,"* or *"It's Ok, I can take it, keep going, I'm here for you,"* or *"if you weren't so damn sexy, I'd leave you alone."*

I remember recently asking my wife a question about something, and she had snapped back for me to *"Google it for myself."* I don't even remember why she was so upset. I went over and playfully whispered in ear, *"I'm going to Google you later on."* It completely broke her pattern because she couldn't help but laugh at my silliness. It changed her mood completely. Who is in charge of the playfulness, the fun, and the light heartedness in your home?

It's easy to engage your partner in a different way, and it's also easy not to. Responses and reactions can be taken far too seriously. **Another example**: My wife was stressed out about a list of things she had to do one night and snapped at me when I asked her to do something for me. She then went into a thirty second rant about all the things she had to do that I didn't seem to see or understand. I simply looked at her and said; *"Ok my little dove."* I had never called her that before in the fourteen years we have been together. It was totally unexpected. We both had a big laugh about it and hugged. Her tension and stress were transformed in the playfulness of the moment that I created. It took two seconds.

Maybe this seems ridiculous to you. Maybe you would never act that way because after all, you are a mature adult.

We all take things way too seriously from time to time. Engage the playful, fun loving, outrageous, silly, and happy go lucky part of yourself from time to time when there is tension in the air. You'll like it and so might your partner!

What can you say that might lighten the mood the next time your partner is upset or frustrated with you?

_____
_____
_____
_____
_____

The tone that you use when you are pushing back is everything. You are pushing softness back into the space that something harsh sounding came from. That harshness cannot survive when it's met with compassion, or silliness, or playfulness, or humor. Don't take my word for it, test it out for yourself and see what happens. I want you to really understand the power that you have to create whatever you want in your relationship.

The next time you find yourself in a disagreement that's escalating with your partner, what can you say that will soften the situation? Hint: Use your heart, not your head . . .

_____
_____

When you know in advance that you can do something to change things in an instant, you give yourself the ability to mend difficult moments quickly. All escalating arguments are based on cycles that typically lack; compassion, heartfelt understanding, creativity, tenderness, and loving empathy. When people fight, they are usually stuck in their heads and not their hearts. When one person gets back to their heart, it can shift the entire situation immediately. Try it, you'll like it!

Can you minimize the button pushing?

Mollie and Jack

Mollie brought her husband Jack in to see me. Even though they arrived together, she just about had to drag him in because he had no interest in working on the relationship with someone else that *didn't get it*. He'd had enough of that in couples counseling a year ago, but he relented because the marriage was just about over.

As we talked about some of the challenges and I was getting his perspective, she interrupted that, "He *was just dragging his old baggage into the relationship*". They had both been married previously and she felt that he was treating her unfairly because of his past hurts. He responded to that with *"You're bringing plenty of baggage into the relationship yourself."* Things went downhill fast. Now it was *the fight to see who had less baggage*. Have you ever been in a similar situation, fighting over something irrelevant and small? *Yes,* is an honest answer that always works really well here.

As I momentarily watched them accuse each other of who brought more baggage into the relationship, I began to get curious about the dynamic between them. She was using very short sentences and so was he. This was like two masculine energies fighting. Someone was out of touch with their core masculine/feminine essence and I was wondering about the polarity until Mollie said . . .

"You're just a lazy bastard". I watched his facial expression tighten significantly and I interrupted with *"I have a question for you Mollie"* before Jack could say anything. Turning to Jack I said;" *Sometimes we say things that aren't helpful to the relationship when we get upset. You have probably said things yourself that haven't been particularly loving from time to time*."

Turning to Mollie, I asked her, "*Was that helpful, useful, or beneficial in creating a loving, passionate, deeply connected relationship?*" Of course, the answer is *no*, it isn't helpful at all, and it isn't useful unless you want to sever the connection, and its impact is certainly not beneficial in any way.

When I examine the specific language and behavior in the relationship, I never say that something is right or wrong, or good or bad. That's the language of blame that people use against each other. I always ask is this helpful, or useful, or beneficial or even supportive to a loving, committed, deeply connected, intimate relationship?

If something is not helpful, then that strategy or tactic needs to be replaced with something that is helpful. From my perspective, removing the right/wrong and good/bad label allows people to make better choices in treating each other. It also significantly minimizes defensiveness around mistakes that everyone makes.

Truly recognize that we all mistakes. People do get triggered, and upset, and stressed out from time to time. No one is perfect or immune from mistakes. We are also so much more than our mistakes. We all have the ability to step up and correct mistakes as we make them. That simply requires getting out of ourselves and back into the importance of the relationship. When you remember what's most important in the heat of any moment it avoids the escalation that ruins good feelings. Remember that section on Vision? What's most important to you, being right, or having a great relationship?

Take a moment to think about your relationship. Looking at your own interaction with your partner, which of your strategies for communication is *not* helpful, not useful, or not beneficial in creating love and connection? Write down some of the things that you're doing now that are *not* creating love and connection in communicating with your partner.

_____
_____
_____
_____
_____
_____

What could you do that would be more helpful, more useful, more beneficial in sustaining connection, love and passion in your relationship communication? Write it here:

_____
_____
_____
_____
_____
_____

I will talk more about name calling and other behaviors that contribute to a hostile environment and the loss of respect that comes with it later on.

Mollie and Jack both acknowledged that their interactions with each other weren't effective strategies for the love and connection that they both desired, and resolved to change it. You can too, because, as I mentioned earlier it is just a choice. It can be easy to do, and it can be incredibly difficult. You can make a new decision right now.

Summary

1. You partner will push your buttons and you will push theirs and upset them.
2. You can interrupt the communication pattern when you respond with softness, or love, or playfulness, or lightness, or compassion. Apologies will also work in case you are wondering.
3. Having heartfelt understanding for your partner puts you into a more effective place for communication. Go there often when communication clashes.
4. We cannot control our partner, so stop trying to do that.
5. We can influence them differently when we come from our hearts and not our heads.

6. One committed person can shift the relationship. It requires a real commitment. Half measures are not effective.
7. Is your communication with your partner, helpful, useful, or beneficial in creating a loving, passionate, deeply connected relationship? If not stop doing it and adopt a different strategy that is helpful, useful, beneficial and supportive in the relationship.

BREAKTHROUGH #6

Tropical Storms

*Your relationship suffers
and so do you when being right becomes
more important than the relationship.*

Tropical Storms

This section is particularly important for men. Getting this part right can make an incredible difference in building and maintaining trust and connection. Taken to a higher level, when the man becomes a safe place for the woman to embrace the totality of her emotional experience, only then will she share fully and open herself completely to her man.

Many women have a fear that if they were to release their full emotional range on a man that he simply couldn't handle it. This is partly true because we men do not understand the emotional range of the feminine. Our emotional range in comparison doesn't do it justice.

Women imagine that men might flee from them after experiencing the first complete outpouring of their full feminine emotions. This belief results in many women trying to keep some of the larger more negative emotions in check as best they can by stuffing them down. This requires extra energy and often results in great frustration. Also, it usually doesn't work because the more something is resisted, the more it tends to persist.

In contrast, while men have a hard time dealing with emotional women, they recognize the passion that exists in emotions. Men aspire to unleash their wild woman in bed who can experience pleasure fully and uninhibitedly. A woman with muted emotions is thought unlikely to be able to offer the responsiveness that keeps us coming back for more.

Unfortunately, keeping up with the unpredictable feminine emotional reactions is an area of challenge and confusion for most men and we tend to get it wrong.

Women experience emotions in a much wider range than men do. We men don't particularly understand this very well because our reference range is narrower.

The chemicals flowing through the female form are different than ours and result in an emotional depth that occasionally leaves us completely bewildered.

For us, these emotional reactions often seem to come out of nowhere with no perceived basis in reality. As a reminder to women, we are merely men after all, and we can't be the mind readers you want us to be all the time. When you are kind enough to give us clues, we do get it right more often than not, and have a much better understanding of what to do that is supportive of you in these situations.

The severity of the emotional reactions can fluctuate with certain times of the month, because when triggered chemically, the intensity increases, and then emotions get less than lovingly released at us. Yes, you know that's true and we men talk about it.

Men feel emotions as well despite what many women think. We have been conditioned to not show and share our feelings. We put on our game face and hide the turmoil going on inside of us. It's in there churning away none the less, whether or not women can see it.

Emotions are energy under pressure. So, women can experience a buildup of pressure as emotions get stacked. All attempts to suppress these emotions have limited success. It usually results in only a delay of the emotional release. However, that delay is unwise because of the intensity that it can bring on the recipient.

This emotional build up and release, or what I call a Tropical Storm, is usually directed at the husband or significant other. What works in addressing these storms, and of our role as men in handling them effectively, is to stand strong and solid like the Rock of Gibraltar, allowing the storm to wash over us. This is something that initially was counter intuitive for me. I had a desire to want to fight back and defend myself. It never worked, so finally I decided to try another approach. I was completely taken by surprise by the effectiveness of standing strong and listening intently.

Once the emotional storm has passed, sunshine and rainbows are sure to follow. Once the emotions are unleashed, if they are let out into a space of acceptance, they tend to wind down relatively quickly. It's the resistance and the defensive fighting back on our part that exacerbates the situation. We men need to learn from our mistakes.

Instructions for men:

Your mission, should you choose to accept it, is to be fully present for your woman. To be able to look her deeply in the eyes and feel what she is experiencing in any Tropical Emotional Storm. *Why bother,* you might ask? Because, it will build a reservoir of trust and without trust, there can be no real intimacy in the relationship. And, because doing this will create an even deeper more connected relationship. Who knows what that feeling of certainty about you being available to understand her might unleash in the bedroom. You can always resist at your own peril and the demise of your intimate connectedness. Be smart men. The rewards are worthwhile.

When you stand strong in the face of the storm you will sense that this emotional outpouring is mostly not about you. Yes, some it will be, but usually it's only a minor piece of the overall picture. The balance is stored emotions that have been under a pressure cooker inside of the female and just need to be released freely. You masculine role is to be the safe place for that?

You will notice, as you hold your ground and allow it to wash over you, that there is much more to it. There's no need to take it personally as an assault on you. There is no need to fight back. There is no need to defend yourself. There is no need to run. You can handle it all. You can even take the greatest hurricane from the place of her deepest fear.

You can remember why you love this woman in this moment, as you listen intently looking deeply into her eyes, giving her your full presence. You can get curious about her and what's really going on emotionally inside of her. You can feel her experience through her eyes as you tune in deeply. You can go beyond the surface emotions and catch a glimpse of who this beautiful, radiant, magnificent woman really is. Then you will know what's real and also what's true.

I remember distinctly the first time that I did this right. I had completely gotten this wrong so many times before. I had grown frustrated by the entire experience. It seemed crazy to me to stand there and take what was coming at me. My instincts were to fight back and defend myself, and to point out how wrong she was. Of course when I did this it only made things worse and escalated the situation. Running for me was never an option.

Finally, out of complete curiosity and tiring of getting it wrong, I decided to do something completely different. Fortunately I didn't listen to my mind say, "W*hy should I put up with this crap.*" Instead, I decided to get curious about what was really happening and do the best I could to figure her out without saying much.

As men know, women have excellent memories, sometimes even creative memories. In these Tropical

Storms, details of disappointment, hurt, or rejection that we men caused years ago will get thrown back at us as if it was thirty seconds ago. You know this to be true.

I remember an emotional storm that my wife had several years ago. She brought up some things from the past including something that I failed to do during her pregnancy five years prior. I had no idea what she was talking about, but I resisted the desire to argue and defend myself. I used one of my more effective responses saying, *"I'm sorry".* I didn't need to say anything more than that while looking deeply into her eyes and feeling her emotions.

My responses continued using limited words. I was just listening and looking at her intently trying to figure the whole thing out. This went on for some minutes with me saying things like, *"Ok,* and *I'm Sorry,* and *you might be right,* and *I understand,* and *I'm here for you,* and *I can take it,* and *I'm not going anywhere, I love you."*

Within a few minutes, she ran out of things to say, and the storm had passed. In those moments she felt understood and reassured that I was committed to her, and that I loved her. In that moment, I truly saw her, and not the superficial argument about nothing. I acknowledged my mistakes and apologized. If you are in any doubt, say, *"I'm sorry."* It's a perfectly acceptable response. There is no need to elaborate. The fewer words the better.

I have also found silence to be very effective if I am looking deeply into her eyes and feeling her. Nodding is good. Shaking your head is not. You can even grunt affirmations if you must. Make sure that you keep deep eye contact at all times.

How have you responded in the past when you experienced a Tropical Emotional Storm directed at you? Did you argue back? Did you defend yourself? Did you escalate the situation? Did you take it personally? Write your old responses here.

_____
_____
_____
_____

Now choose how you will respond to the next Tropical Storm. What's your plan? You better have one because while they do get easier, they do not stop entirely. I struggled a bit with this realization. They lessen considerably in intensity but do surface from time to time. Plan ahead and know exactly what to do. It will give you total peace of mind. Now write your plan here.

_____
_____
_____
_____
_____

A few personal examples:

A slight squall

While having dinner at home with my wife and son some years ago, my wife asked me how I liked my salad. It seemed innocent enough. On the surface, a reasonable question, because she had just made her own version of a salmon salad that we had both enjoyed from a recent restaurant visit.

Now, I usually understand feminine communication well, but being the clueless male that I am from time to time, I was caught off guard, involved in a side conversation with my son and not really paying attention.

I turned to her and replied, "I like the vegetables cut a little smaller." For me in that moment, it was the right answer to a simple question. Big mistake! I had not looked closely enough at her before I answered the question.

I had failed a test of masculine energy. I had not been present with her.

I had not realized it was really a different question. One that was deeper, and hiding within it a reason for a storm to appear. She was asking me if I appreciated her in my life and her gesture of trying to make me happy.

If I had answered it correctly, she would not have snapped, "*Nothing is ever good enough for you.*" Now she has my attention, and catching up fast I realized that I had answered the wrong question. So I chose to say nothing despite an energy rising of "*What the F*ck are you talking about?*"

I knew that for her, the best thing for me to do in that moment was to let her have her space and the tiny little storm would pass, and of course it did. If I had chosen to react to her tone, as I have in the past, who knows where it would have gone; certainly no place supportive to the relationship. It might have been the prelude to a full blown hurricane.

If the emotional storm was larger, of the Tropical variety, I would have done something very different, because I do understand how feminine energy communicates . . . most of the time.

In an attempt to be open with her feminine energy and vulnerability, she had trusted me enough to test me and my masculine energy with the following unspoken thoughts:

Is what I am doing for you good enough? Am I enough for you? Can you accept me unconditionally even when I am scared and emotional? Will you reject me? Can you see how much I love you by this gesture to please you? Can you see how important it is in this moment to reassure me that I am ok, and to give me your total attention? Do you love me?

If you are a man reading this you are probably saying *"Huh! You've got to be kidding me".* If you are a feminine woman, you're probably smiling and totally relating to this situation. For this woman, if I were to have done it right, I would have looked her deeply in the eyes and said *"Thank you. The salad is really great. I really appreciate you . . . making it for me. I love you."* I would also have kept looking in her eyes to see if she had anything else to say, and to check in on her reaction.

This emotional storm ended quickly because I didn't argue with her. I didn't get upset at her making a massive generalization that had no basis in fact for me. I accepted where she was emotionally and responded in a way that was helpful to the relationship.

I chose not to respond by arguing and trying to prove myself right. I chose not to pick apart her words. I chose not to defend myself. All of those responses would have escalated the situation. Something I had no interest in doing.

I want to have an amazing relationship, so I chose to do what would minimize the damage in the moment of my screw up. My marriage is more important than any moment of misunderstanding.

Admitting I had made a mistake is going to puzzle some men. *How is there a mistake in answering a simple question with an honest answer,* you might ask? The mistake was in misinterpreting where she was at emotionally in that moment, because I wasn't paying full attention to her. That's usually the mistake that men make.

The other aspect of the mistake was in not giving her my presence with my answer. This was a minor mistake. You can begin to understand the consequences of misunderstanding feminine communication. The connection between any couple can easily be severed over time, even with small things such as this example.

The bigger mistake would have been to defend myself which would have immediately resulted in an escalation of emotions and words. After realizing I had messed up, I chose the best response for the relationship by placing it above my ego. I chose to do something that was helpful, useful and beneficial to the relationship.

Some thoughts and ideas for women:

Your emotional experience is important and I humbly suggest you honor that part of you. To feel fully is the feminine gift. In these feelings is incredible wisdom about what you need in any moment. You don't need any man to make you happy. You need to be happy with you, by yourself. The man's role is to make you *happier*. You must fill yourself up with self care first and then you become more available to everyone around you. How you choose to do that in a way that supports you is always available.

When you try to suffocate and minimize the emotional experience a part of you becomes empty. This doesn't serve you at all. I have seen this emptiness countless times in clients. It blocks joy from existing within you. Embrace your totality and you will find bliss.

Women are kicking ass and taking names in all aspects of society. Women are rising to the top and are competing equally with men for the highest positions and rightly so because you are more than capable.

The challenge for women today is to return to your heart. To get back in touch with the feminine core that will complete you, to reconnect with your intuition that you sense so fully and perhaps aren't listening to. Many of you have forgotten about it, or have chosen to ignore it because of some mistake in the past. Let them go. You are not your mistakes and you are bigger than any mistake that you could ever have made.

I have worked with many executive and professional women over the last seven years. All were feeling unhappy and unfulfilled despite great career and financial success. When I helped them reconnect to their hearts and core feminine nature, they became happier than they had been in years. Some saying they were happier than ever before in their lives. They had all perceived femininity as weakness and in order to compete with men, they had abandoned a part of themselves.

While these women were highly successful, it had come at heavy cost; their personal happiness.

My role in helping women get back in touch with their hearts and feminine totality has been interesting. This isn't something that I set out to do. It actually came as quite a shock to me. I stumbled upon this by accident, trying to help one of the most aggressive women that I had ever met, because client results matter to me.

Claire's story

Claire's company sent her to see me because she needed an attitude adjustment. She had been in a senior management position for a Fortune 500 company and had been told that she would lose her position unless she was able to change her management style. She struggled to get along with her co-workers and it was creating a significant morale problem. This was her final warning.

Claire was angry. I introduced myself and sat at my conference room table. She sat on the edge of her chair across from me and leaned way out into the middle of the table toward me. She had both elbows on the table, arms fully extended, and fists clenched. I was a bit taken aback. Her body language and posture indicated a high state of aggression.

Wow, I thought, *if this was a man, this would be trouble and very likely a provocation.* It was kind of like someone poking you in the chest. My space had been fully invaded, and none too gently. You could feel the anger pouring out of her. My curiosity was on high alert.

Not only was Claire angry and unhappy, she had been sent to see a man to get her attitude fixed and she didn't trust men. Her job was on the line and she knew nothing about me. She had been given an ultimatum and had no choice in the matter if she wanted to keep her job.

She didn't want to be there, and said so a number of times. She certainly didn't want to hear anything that I had to say. It was an interesting beginning. I thought that this was the most masculine woman that I had ever met until I took another look at her and said, "T*ell me about anger."*

Claire was dressed in a black suit with no makeup, jewelry or earrings. I noticed that she wore red nail polish; a tiny splash of color on a very unhappy canvas. *Was it a splash of feminine,* I thought to myself. *Was she completely shifted away from her core feminine nature for some reason?"* My intuition would prove me right.

Sometimes, I pick up on client core issues quickly. How or why, I have no idea, and it doesn't matter. I rely fully and completely on my intuition in my coaching work despite being a very masculine man because it serves me so well. I have found that I am more effective if I pay less attention to the thoughts in my head and focus more on what feels right in the moment. I highly recommend it. We all use masculine and feminine energy unknowingly. When we are conscious of it, we all can become more effective.

Claire had adopted the masculine energy to raise four children by herself, and to support a minimally working, troubled husband. She had taken on the role to survive. She had been successful financially and in her career. It had served her in many ways. The problem was, she was completely unhappy with herself and that unhappiness was now wreaking havoc at work.

I taught Claire how to add femininity back into her life as an experiment. She hated flowers, so I told her that she had to have flowers on her desk at work every day. My intention was to see how she felt after a number of days into the experiment. I was simply testing my theory and had no idea if it would work or not. I had no shortage of other ideas that I was willing to test as the process continued.

I asked Claire to simply notice what she was feeling, nothing more than that. Just noticing how she was feeling with the flowers around her day to day. I was interested only in how her feelings might change or not change at all. My entire approach was one of curiosity. I had no idea what was going to work, but I was willing to try anything to find out.

I also had her add splashes of pink to her accessories which she initially also hated. I added jewelry and brighter colored clothing, and scented baths and massage, reflexology, and lingerie, etc. I had no idea what specifically would work for her, so I suggested quite a variety of things as part of my experiment. All that I focused on was how she felt with something new, not my specific ideas. Claire would ultimately decide which of these ideas to keep for herself and which ones to reject. It was always up to her.

She agreed to it all, because she liked the idea of the experiment and that she wasn't obligated to keep any of my suggestions. She could throw them all out whenever she wanted.

Some weeks later, I taught Claire how to access the wisdom of her heart, and watched the tears fall. She hadn't cried in a very long time and said she didn't cry. Over the next several months, I watched her transform in front of my eyes into a powerful feminine woman. All of her resistance had vanished. She had demonstrated incredible courage with me by trusting me. While she resisted me initially, we had come a long way from our first meeting and I had earned her trust.

She had done everything that I had asked her to do. My wild experiment had succeeded and I had benefited greatly by witnessing one of the greatest transformations in my coaching work. I had also gained some remarkable insights that I would use over and over again with dozens of highly successful, career driven professional women.

The results were all hers. She had done it. She was happier than she had ever been. I felt honored to have been able to participate in her inspiring transformation.

Her work situation had shifted direction and was going well. Her peers and co-workers were reaching out to her for guidance which was a huge change. Some of her co-workers went out of their way to tell her boss how helpful she was to them. This wouldn't have been possible before our work together. She was genuinely happy at work now because she felt free to be herself.

She had discovered a higher magnitude of influence over the people around her because she was now accessing more effective resources for her situation.

Her troubled relationship with her boyfriend had also changed. He had gone from being in and out of her life to committing fully to her. The best change however, was that she truly loved herself now and was happier than she had ever been.

What role are you playing today? Are you in a masculine or a feminine role? Are you wearing a mask to be someone you really are not? Who are you at your core? Are you a masculine woman or a feminine woman? How do you know for certain?

_____
_____
_____
_____
_____

How connected are you to your heart and feelings? Are you able to hear the whispers of wisdom that come from your intuition? How often do you honor that part of you? Describe how you do that here.

_____
_____
_____

What do you do that makes you feel good? How do you pamper yourself, and fill yourself up with feminine energy? How often?

What prevents you from being happier in your life? What keeps you from happiness?

What are you going to do about it? What will you do to get more in touch with you?

As a woman, you can take responsibility for you reactions. You can learn how to come from your heart more often instead of your head. Your mind will fill you with all kinds of thoughts that really don't serve you. Ever notice that? This small distinction will generate an enormous difference in communication effectiveness. Try it and see for yourself.

Is it time to take off your masculine mask that serves you in certain roles but not in others? You can always put it back on when you need it. How will you know when to do that?

The feminine is found in your heart and intuition. So is profound insight and wisdom. This is the place to spend more of your time and feel what it's like to be there, and notice its' impact on you and those around you.

Tropical Hurricane Clean Up

Here's an example of how easy it is to ruin your relationship. From time to time in the past, I was really good at it. Due to some frustration over the course of a few weeks, I decided to use a date night, car ride to the movies as a time to have a conversation with my wife about what she was doing wrong in our relationship. Yup, you already know this isn't going to go well. I'm only a man after all.

Please forgive me my moments of ignorance. They will happen again.

I was frustrated with her and had been reminding her about how she was dropping the ball on some things that were really important to me. Huge things! Well, not really. Ok, these little tiny things kept stacking up on top of each other and it seemed like they became big things. This is usually what happens that creates a chasm between couples.

Anyway, in my wisdom of the moment, I had elaborated on how she was creating additional stress on me and our son. (I told you I was good at this). She immediately got defensive, frustrated and angry . . . hardly a surprise to anyone reading this now.

I continued to push her about how she needed to change, and do the things that I was talking about. And of course the more I pushed, the more upset she got. In those moments, I had forgotten something very important. No woman wants to be told by any man that she needs fixing, or that she's doing something wrong unless the timing is right and the tone is loving. Even with the right tone, at the right time, this is hazardous territory.

I had made multiple mistakes over the span of a few minutes. Why stop at one mistake when you can make more? So, now she says, "T*ake me home and don't talk to me, I want to be alone."* This is where I finally start to recover a brain cell or two. It was about time, and it was also too late.

I continue to drive towards the movies saying nothing. She says nothing and her body language suggests that I had become some kind of bacteria she wanted to avoid at all costs. I'm sure some you men reading this have been there.

We arrive at the movies and I suggest to her that she go the movie that she had wanted to see and I would go see another movie playing at the same time, and we would meet after. That way she could spend some time alone. She accepted this crumb from me without acknowledgement, other than walking by herself towards the front door of the theater.

Now I have two hours to think about how I had totally screwed that whole thing up, and what I was going to do about it while I'm trying to watch a great movie. That sucked! Have you ever been there? It's hard to focus completely on the movie because you still have this fight in your head and need to figure out what to do next.

We meet after our movies and her body language toward me suggests that I have some deadly contagious disease she wants to avoid at all costs. We get into the car, and I tell her that I want to talk to her for a few minutes. Her facial expression and tension indicate zero interest in this. I tell her that I want to talk about me, and not her. She relaxes a bit and says ok.

I tell her that I have a lot going on with a crazy work schedule, and that I had certain expectations of her which were totally unfair, and that I was sorry about that. I tell her that I am not perfect and that I mess up a lot, just like our conversation a few hours ago, and say I'm very sorry. I tell her I love her, and that I was thinking about going into her movie to join her. She says she wished I had. The mood has been shifted because my conversation is from my heart and I have smartened up talking about what's real for me.

I say that I had thought about being alone without her in my life, and no matter how difficult a moment might be that I wanted to be with her always. She says that she thought the same thing. I tell her how committed I am to our relationship and how it breaks my heart when she does X and Y. The impact of this is different. Now of course, I have her full attention, and the conversation gets much better. We are hugging and she apologizes for her part in the argument. This is a bonus for me because I was completely happy to claim one hundred percent responsibility for my ridiculousness. She had stepped up and surprised me again.

I talk with her about being aligned and we talk about what we want from each other. Everything ends really well, and we are back to normal, actually a little better than our normally great relationship. This difficulty reinforces our commitment to each other and our love because we worked it out. It creates a slightly higher level of solidness to our relationship foundation which is kind of amazing. That will not happen unless you truly own your mistakes.

This is not the ideal way to go about achieving a higher level of connectedness, and I wouldn't recommend it, but it's a good example of how you can recover from any mistake if you choose to. This isn't always an easy choice to make because the past can get in our way.

This was more of a category 5 hurricane than a tropical storm, but the relationship hadn't just survived, it had gained more trust, more security, and more connection from my perspective. I had grown in the process of discomfort because I had chosen to face it. It would have been easier to say, *Screw it, look at all the things she's not doing for me.*"

I view my role in the relationship as the leader, and as a leader I choose to go first. I choose to set the example, and the tone of the relationship. I choose to step up and reach out to restore the connection first. I apologize first. Why? Because I want to create something amazing based on my vision and I work toward that every day in between the occasional screw up. Who leads in your relationship?

We all get caught up in ourselves and what we aren't getting from time to time. Relationships can be really challenged in the fight for whose needs are more important. It's me, me, and me first sometimes isn't it. We all have been there.

Even great relationships have fragile moments, because we all make mistakes. What are you willing to do when things go wrong? It takes a lot more than just knowing what to do. It requires a willingness to actually do something about it. If you want a great relationship, you must be willing to do the things that can be difficult and uncomfortable. That takes courage.

It's easy to shut your partner out and put up walls. It takes no effort at all. But to reach out to them to initiate repairing the relationship, apologizing even if you think you're right, is the courage that heals more than that moment. It's part mastery of self, a strength that lasts a lifetime. The payoff is enormous in terms of building trust and connection. When your partner realizes that the relationship is truly important to you, they will surprise you with their willingness to demonstrate their commitment as well. My wife surprises me frequently.

Take a moment now to consider what you are really committed to in your relationship. Write it here:

_____
_____
_____
_____
_____
_____
_____
_____

If you want to criticize your partner, or tell them what they're doing wrong. The tone has to be soft, much softer than your normal tone. Even softer than you are thinking now, because your normal tone will actually sound harsh when you tell someone they aren't doing something right. Your tone is vitally important, because we all have defense mechanisms that kick in naturally when someone criticizes us. If you come totally and genuinely from your heart you will have found the right tone.

Summary

1. Women's emotional range is larger than men's and can be prone to tropical emotional storms as suppressed emotions need to escape from time to time.
2. Men experience lots of emotions but rarely show them.
3. Men need to understand that emotional storms are a normal and necessary part of the feminine.
4. Women need to allow their emotional experience instead of using valuable energy to keep emotions in check. This would result in less intense emotional storm release.
5. Men's role in any storm is to stand strong, look their partner in the eyes with their full presence of attention and tune into what's really going on beyond any words.
6. The Masculine presence builds trust. Men can become a safe place for the feminine to experience their fullness and as a result build a deeper level of connection and intimacy with their partner.
7. When the Masculine presence is a safe place for the Feminine to be fully herself, she will open more completely to her man.

8. When women lose touch with their hearts, they lose touch with an important aspect of the feminine often resulting in unhappiness.
9. Relationships thrive when women understand how important it is that they are happy themselves. The man's role is to make them happier through the relationship.
10. Real and genuine communication from the emotional heart is where relationship upsets heal, not from the intellectual mind.

BREAKTHROUGH #7

Me First or Maybe Not

*When your life is about significance,
it's difficult to have a happy marriage.
Just ask any celebrity. No one wins in the fight
for whose needs are more important.*

Me First or Maybe Not

Do you remember why you are in a relationship to begin with? If it's simply a place to get unconditional love you will be sadly disappointed. When you first fell totally in love, you would have done anything to make your partner happy. How quickly things can change.

Resentment, hurt feelings, keeping score, anger, disappointment and a host of other emotions keep people from wanting to give to their partners. They tell me, "*He/she has to do something for me first, and then I will give to them.*" Usually what happens is that both partners remain stuck in the attitude of "*they have to go first, because they owe me,*" so nothing changes.

If you are in a relationship to get without being willing to give first, your relationship will be painful and you will struggle to find happiness. I hear lots of *me, me, me*. It's always about *me* when you're not getting what you want. It can be tough to feel like giving when you haven't gotten anything for long periods of time. What's also tough is relationship stress. What's tougher is divorce. What's toughest of all is the pain of regret.

People tell themselves soft lies. I often hear, "B*ut I've tried everything,*" and "*I've given them everything.*" These seem true on the surface, but the reality is different. They might be giving everything other than what the other person needs. For example, "*I told her I loved her every day and she claimed I didn't love her.*" Maybe the way she wanted to experience love was through touch or through a gesture, and because you gave love verbally saying, "*I love you,*" the way *you* wanted to receive it, she never felt loved.

In my private practice, I have replaced the old Golden Rule—*Treat others the way you want to be treated* with my own updated version: *Treat others the way they prefer to be treated*. The way that you want to be treated may have little to do with what your partner really wants when it comes to relationships. That means you'd better know what your partner needs in the way that they really need it.

People might think that they've tried everything, but when I ask for the specifics of what was done, I find that most people have tried only three or four different things, and then give up quickly when nothing changes. Is our creativity that limited? What happened to our willingness to do whatever it takes? What happened to our determination to figure it out?

If it was truly important wouldn't we make more of a persistent commitment? Wouldn't we explore every possibility? That's what's really required if you want something to change. We need to stop taking the easy way out and rationalizing that we did everything we could do. The need for instant gratification has taken our focus off of what's important long term and we are paying the price emotionally, physically and financially.

What's missing in most relationships? In my observations of clients, I frequently see; low levels of commitment, a lack of determination, very little creativity, and not much playfulness or fun. We have forgotten laughter. There's no sense of adventure, no courage, no compassion, and what happened to the focused persistence to make our life's priorities successful? It also takes a real willingness to do something different when what we are doing doesn't work out. What was your commitment level, again?

Your relationship is not a disaster because you don't understand your partner. It's a mess because you haven't stepped up and become more determined and committed to either figure it out by trial and error, or to pursue the real help that you need.

Your communication with your partner is a struggle not so much because you don't understand the opposite sex, it's because you haven't had the creativity to playfully engage your partner differently.

I find that the effort people are making to ignite passion to be fairly low on their list of priorities. You can't demand passion, you have to entice it with fun, and play, and lightheartedness, and sensual curiosity.

I have discovered that many people are looking for the easy way out when faced with the reality that the relationship requires a real commitment. There are so many other things that get in the way because of our busy, stress—filled lives. I have had many people ask me to fix their partners as a way of evading all responsibility in the relationship. After all, it couldn't be that *they* personally had any role in the demise of the relationship.

I heard a great quote from Satyen Raja, a friend of mine who focuses on bringing out passion in couples. He says, *"Ignite passion now! Because everything else can wait!"* It's so true! Everything else can wait when the relationship's success is the central ingredient in overall happiness and life success. However, most of us aren't living that way.

Let's explore what keeps individuals from being the one who gives first when relationships are stressed:

Here are some samples of the thought process I see:

What if I were to give my partner everything, and open up fully and meet all of their needs? What about me? That leaves me exposed and vulnerable. What if I gave every day and then I got nothing back? All that work, for nothing. That would be the ultimate rejection. I can't take that risk. They have to go first; I'm tired of giving to them. I always go first. They need to change if this marriage is going to work, etc.

So, the alternative is to hang back and let the relationship die a slow torturous death, and to inflict emotional turmoil on the children and family members, to contribute to an already stressful household with far reaching consequences affecting health and longevity. It becomes ok to self destruct the financial well being of a family. Does this alternative really make sense?

According to Forbes, as of 2012 there are about 1,200 billionaires in the world. What percentage do you think are married? Take a wild guess. The actual number of married billionaires is about ninety percent. When you dig into the numbers as I have done, these people are making better decisions up front in selecting a life partner, and then they bring the same tenacity to the relationship that they bring into the business world. They don't give up when things get tough. They become more committed, and more determined to make things work. What about you?

Marriage builds wealth. Successful relationships create a solid foundation at home that becomes a spring board for calculated risk taking at work, which is the true key to financial abundance. It's no secret that divorce is devastating on wealth.

It's hard to think of consequences for everyone involved when we are totally focused on ourselves. The fear of rejection and the fear of not being enough can severely limit our willingness to do what the relationship requires from us.

Fear is what holds us back. Fear prevents us from being able to give what's needed in the relationship. Another one of these fears is the loss of self. Some people believe that they will deplete themselves fully in the relationship until there is nothing left. I have heard, *"I will lose me if I do that." "I'm afraid that I won't be me anymore."* It's just an illusion based on a mindset of scarcity about who we really are.

Fear prevents us from seeing the reality of the impact of a failed marriage. As I had mentioned earlier, children of divorce have a significantly greater likelihood of divorcing when they get married. Who wants this legacy? The emotional trauma alone can create long term unhappiness and depression for some people. The consequences of not figuring it out are painfully high.

When people realize that they have the resourcefulness inside to do everything that's needed, then things can change. When they bring an attitude of playful curiosity to figure their partner out, lots of good things can happen fast.

Who gives first in a great relationship? Your best answer is *"I do!"* It's also the best answer from your partner. That indicates that you both see the needs of the other as equal to your own. It means that you see the relationship's success as equal to or greater in importance than your own self interests.

This requires courage. It's easy not to do this. It's easy to get caught up in what you aren't getting. It takes no courage to feel hurt or bitter. It takes no guts to hold onto a past hurt for eleven years and let it keep you from contributing to the relationship. Even most crimes have a statute of limitations. Your partner probably deserves the same courtesy.

People have incredible courage. They can choose to forgive their partners. They can choose to value the relationship more than their own needs. They can choose to value love over the certainty of *playing it safe . . . just in case*. They can choose to be role models for the children and to create an environment of appreciation for each other. But, all of those things require courage.

Frank and Jo Anne

Jo Anne came to see me about boosting her confidence for a new job that she was taking in management. She told me that her marriage was ending and that she wasn't feeling good about herself at all. She had been severely stressed out over the loss of love and had just found herself a new place to live and would be moving out within the month.

I asked Jo Anne if she wanted to work on the relationship. She told me that she and Frank had been to couples counseling and that he had given up after a few months. He said it was a complete waste of time and she admitted that it wasn't going anywhere.

Frank had been to an attorney and drawn up divorce papers. He had blamed the relationship failure on her because she had never been able to trust him fully. Frank didn't want to see me at all but I asked him to meet with me so that he could look himself in the mirror and know that he had done everything he could before he moved on.

Frank didn't believe it was possible to make the marriage work. He believed the problems were entirely her fault. He suggested that if I could *fix her* then he would reconsider the relationship because he did still love her.

I met with Frank and Jo Anne so that he could leave with a totally clear conscience. Frank suggested that Jo Anne was damaged because of childhood traumas. Jo Anne agreed that she was still bothered by some of it.

The relationship dynamic was very interesting. Jo Anne was extremely feminine and Frank seemed to be very masculine but somehow the relationship wasn't working at all. Frank fought with Jo Anne all the time, fighting her constant questions and refusing to explain himself or his whereabouts. This, of course, made Jo Anne more and more uncertain about the relationship and magnified the cycle of questioning and evading. It was easy to understand what was really happening. How can you trust a man who won't answer your questions or is always defending himself?

From Frank's perspective, how could he relax when he is always being grilled about his where abouts? How could he accept the constant questioning of his every move?

I explained to Frank that a feminine woman like Jo Anne needs a strong man in her life to provide for her certainty, and because of her past she may need an even stronger man. I challenged him with the following, "*This is clearly a very feminine woman and the only real question is, are you man enough to handle her? Are you man enough to be that strong, to be her unshakeable rock?*" I told Frank that perhaps she needed a stronger man in her life. Of course, this pissed him off and he wanted to know where I would get such a ridiculous idea.

It was the only time I saw the couple. They left with a long list of things to consider that we had discussed. Jo Anne called me several days later and said that something had changed with Frank and that she was feeling much happier and had decided not to move out. I never spoke to Frank again, but Jo Anne kept in touch with me on and off for over a year letting me know how things were going. Frank had dropped the divorce idea within two weeks and had recommitted to Jo Anne and they were doing great, as of her last report.

I believe that anything is possible when it comes to repairing relationships if you get to the core issues. I have seen my theory proven over and over again. The greatest difficulty exists when one person has completely given up, moved on emotionally, and has shut off contact with the other person.

Elizabeth

Elizabeth called me distraught that her husband had filed for divorce and was moving out to be with another woman. She was more upset about losing him than she was about the affair. I talked with her about how to handle that, as well as how to handle every interaction that they would have with each other. I told her that she needed to be happy when she was around her husband, and appreciative of him at every opportunity to do so.

She admitted that she hadn't done that in years and that it would be hard for her to do.

The couple had two children, so there would be plenty of brief interactions that would allow him to see the real

Elizabeth and not the hurt, needy, miserable Elizabeth. Of course her friends and family were giving her much different guidance. They were telling her to move on and have as little to do with him as possible other than making financial demands. She told me that she loved him and wanted him back and would forgive him. So that was the goal we worked towards.

Elizabeth's husband moved out and moved in with his girl friend a few weeks later. After about six weeks with her, he left and moved in with a male friend. He had begun telling all of his friends that he had made a mistake and would be reuniting with Elizabeth. Unfortunately, that never happened because he died in a tragic car accident.

Elizabeth called me with the heart breaking news and wanted me to know that the things I asked her to do had worked. She had known he was going to come home to her.

Love cannot wait. There isn't time. Life will shake us to our very core when we least expect it. What's really important to you? Commit to it now! Love fully now and live your life without regrets.

So who goes first in your relationship? Who reaches out first after an argument? What do you do when things are difficult or there is tension between you and your partner? Write it here:

_____
_____
_____
_____
_____

Maybe it's time to do something that is more helpful, beneficial and useful for the success of the relationship. Here's your chance to decide to change your approach. What will you do now to initiate the repair of the marriage? How quickly will you decide that this is really important to your happiness and life success?

Now that you are going to be the one to go first, what are you willing to do that might be more effective when there are inter personal struggles? Write it here:

_____
_____
_____
_____
_____

When I work with a couple, I ask each of them to accept one hundred percent responsibility for the relationship. It's not enough to take fifty percent responsibility. When people do that, they find themselves calculating whose turn it is to go first. What are you waiting for?

In my marriage, I am perfectly ok with going first every time. I am perfectly fine with being the one to step up every single time and own the total responsibility of the relationship. Why? Because I want to make my vision come true. I want to live it right now and this gives me the ability to progress toward that every single time.

As a result of my willingness to go first, my wife also steps up from time to time. For me this is an unexpected pleasure. It always seems to catch me by surprise because I'm not looking for it. My willingness is not contingent on her doing anything. We are able to bring each other slices of happiness in unexpected ways. You can do this too!

If you are trying to shift a relationship by yourself, I want you to know that you need to *give* to meet your partner's needs *first* without expecting anything in return for a period of time . . . maybe ninety days. Your job is to just give them what they need to the best of your ability every day, and desire nothing back. Your mindset has to be that you want, and need nothing from your partner for that period of time.

This isn't easy. In fact it's difficult. You may question why you are doing this for the first few weeks. It's harder than you might think. There is this part of us that gets impatient and says, *What about me. Nothing is happening and it's been 3 whole days."* (Yes, a client actually said that) *What's wrong with them, this is bull shit, etc.* It's much easier if you have someone to guide you through this process than going it alone.

What's in it for you if you do this? Their needs will get met, and you will also get what you really want, just a few weeks or months later. The ultimate *what's in it for you* is that you have a chance to elevate and even transform your relationship. You have an opportunity to create an incredible relationship that your friends will envy. You might become happier than you have ever been in your life.

You already know what happens if you do nothing, or can't figure it out.

This process requires a commitment. It can be difficult to put your personal needs behind someone else's needs. It's difficult to subordinate yourself for the sake of the relationship. If it was easy, there would be so many more great marriages.

While it's typical for people to notice some changes right away, sometimes the person doing all the giving can have feelings of resentment because they see nothing coming back for a few weeks or more. This is such a short window of giving in the context of what's at stake and also considering the amount of time that couples have spent with each other. You can do it easily if you choose. I have done it myself, and suggest it often with clients who are on the edge.

Your relationship is in your hands. You get to decide what you want that to be like and then go make it happen. You have incredible power to influence the relationship. Will you in a way that's helpful, beneficial and supportive?

Choice points occur all the time in relationships. When your partner is upset or stressed about something how will you choose to react? If your partner wants to argue with you about something totally ridiculous how will you choose to respond? If your partner is talking unkindly to you, what will you choose to say? If your partner blames you for everything wrong in the relationship what will you do? Make a decision that benefits or helps the relationship . . . or not . . . you always get to decide.

If you decide to go first, you will notice some interesting things right away. I want you to test these strategies for yourself. Don't say, *"I get it, I understand,"* because you intellectually comprehend what you have read here. Go do something! Change happens because people do things, not because they think about things. Pondering can be a form of procrastination.

Discover what happens for yourself when you give first. It's always a choice. Which will you choose?

Summary

1. One partner has to go first or nothing happens.
2. That partner should be you.
3. Take one hundred percent responsibility for the relationship.
4. Get more creative, more committed, more determined, more courageous, etc.
5. Choose to do what's beneficial to the relationship to the best of your ability.
6. Make a decision to take action. Go do something today to shift your relationship.
7. Anything is possible no matter how dire a situation might appear if you are willing to truly go after what you want.
8. Knowledge is great, but nothing happens unless you *do* something.
9. Choose to do something and now do it.

BONUS #1

The Magic of Courage

What makes it easy for couples to separate is a lack of determination to make it work or figure it out . . . People leave by giving up.

The Magic of Courage

Marriages fail all the time. It's not because of a lack of love; it's often because of a lack of something else. No, not sex although lots of marriages lack sex.

When you look at the reality of marriage today, my best guess is that about ten to fifteen percent of marriages are happy. Happy doesn't mean that things are just ok. Happy marriages fill the hearts of the couple.

A happy marriage means that you are still in love with and feel a deep connection and passion for your partner. It means your life is enhanced is so many ways because of your marriage and you feel grateful to have that person to share your life with. After 14 years together, that's where I am in my marriage. Do you know many people who are really happily married?

Why do so many couples struggle? There's plenty information out there about what to do to fix your relationship. I have a free report on my website loaded with content that works fast. I constantly refer people to it who cannot afford my guidance. But, very few actually look at it. Do they connect with me hoping for the one sentence relationship cure all? Everyone wants the magic pill, the easy way out, the no personal responsibility solution.

Here's the truth: Marriage isn't easy. Marriage can be difficult. Any long term relationship can have challenging moments. Being with another person isn't always perfectly fun. There will be occasional struggles even in the most loving relationships.

What do people do in those difficult moments? From my own observations, they seem to be doing very little. How are people responding to the ongoing challenges in their relationships? In my experience they are mostly responding poorly.

Here's why: What people lack is not love, it's not information, it's *courage.*

It takes courage to put your partner first. It takes courage to make your marriage more important than something else in your busy life. It takes courage to have heart felt understanding for your partner. It takes courage to admit you are wrong and apologize. It takes real courage to want something exceptional and have the willingness to do something all the time to make that happen. It takes courage to reach out for help.

It takes courage to step into the difficult and uncomfortable thing and to do it even when it's really tough and you don't want to, and you are afraid. Maybe you are afraid of rejection, afraid of not being enough, afraid of giving and not getting anything back. Facing all of those fears and doing it anyway requires courage. Courage is the willingness to continue to pursue solutions when it looks like the end.

This is not to say that every marriage should be saved. There are times when couples have grown apart, or harmful circumstances legitimately indicate that people should separate, or the partner's life views are no longer compatible.

Here's a suggestion that I gave a woman recently who was going through a tough time and was at odds with her partner:

"Maybe John is feeling off because he doesn't know how to handle you right now and you are feeling strange because you don't know how you feel about him exactly.

If you decided that you were going to ask him to hold you for a few moments, and know he might reject you and ask him to anyway, and know that he might want to say something you wouldn't want to hear, or that he might be confused, and still allow that to happen, knowing that it was hard to do anyway, and then what if he agrees to hold you, and to find something in that holding that could create a new moment. That requires courage. Doing it and knowing it may not happen the way you want, and doing it anyway, because if it works, it will be so worthwhile . . . maybe incredibly comforting . . . maybe re-connecting . . . maybe even a magic moment.

That's courage in action, and your willingness to step into your courage and do that over and over again knowing it might fail, and knowing that you never fail when you are addressing fear, creates a strength that can't be taken away."

This is how marriages get transformed, one act of courage at a time. This is how relationships get changed. This is how couples can immediately reconnect. Find the courage to do the thing that's difficult more often and everything can change. The more you do this, the easier and easier it becomes. And right now is a great time to start.

What is the courageous thing that your marriage/relationship needs the most from you?

_____
_____
_____
_____
_____

Is there anything that you need to apologize for? Do you need to reach out to your partner and say something that might heal your relationship? What might change if you did this courageous thing?

Rebecca

Rebecca talked with me about the struggles she and her husband were experiencing. She hadn't felt connected with him for a long time. They didn't seem to be aligned on very much including the discipline of the children.

As we talked, I asked her about how decisions were made in the household. Rebecca and her husband had three children that were very close in age and she was used to arbitrarily deciding what was happening with them. She scheduled all of their activities and organized their lives. This decisiveness was far reaching. She controlled the family money, she controlled the investments, she controlled the social activities, and she controlled every aspect of the family's life. There was very little her husband had any say over and she fought with him frequently to maintain this control. The friction had increased to a breaking point.

Rebecca admitted that whatever she was doing wasn't working. The relationship was in turmoil. She had taken on the masculine energy in the relationship and was now in a constant struggle to maintain it. The more she fought, the worse she felt. The more she battled to remain in control of everything, the more she felt separate from her man.

Based on our conversation, Rebecca decided to do the most difficult thing she could imagine. She went home and apologized to her husband for not treating him with the respect that he deserved. She apologized for wanting to control him, and said that she never wanted him to feel like she had all the power. She apologized for taking him for granted for the last few years. She asked for his help and input making decisions for the family. This took great courage.

She reported back to me that he was, "*completely shocked and thrilled,*" by her surprising change of heart. An enormous weight had been lifted from her and a gift had been given to him. She was able to open herself and be vulnerable with him for the first time in years. The discomfort of facing this fear was perhaps the most beneficial thing she could ever have done to restore the relationship.

What's possible when you step into your courage? What would happen in your relationship if you apologized out of the blue for past wrongs or misunderstandings, or for neglecting your partner's real needs? Do you have the courage it takes to just do it?

What act of courage will you commit to doing right now?

_____
_____
_____
_____
_____

So now go do it.

Another personal story

A few years ago I came to the realization that many women I had worked with were disappointed with their husbands. Over the course of years, I had heard story after story of how the men had fallen short of expectations and disappointed their wives in so many different ways. I began to wonder if in fact I had also disappointed my wife. I knew on some level it was likely true and that I needed to do something about it. I am certain that I'm not always easy to love and understand. I have my moments and you have read a few of them earlier.

I realized that I needed to own up to my shortcomings in our relationship. The next day I told my wife that I wanted to apologize to her for disappointing her or neglecting her in any way over the years. I said that it wasn't intentional, and I hadn't been aware of all of it, but I had been thinking that there were times that I had been really difficult and that I had made many mistakes. I told her that I was sorry and would work on my interactions with her in the future.

Did I need to do this? No. Was this uncomfortable for me? Yes, because it would give her a chance to tell me that I wasn't a good enough husband. It would give her an opportunity to agree and tell me about all of the times I had let her down. It would give her an opportunity to reveal any harboring of ill will toward me. It might open a can of worms that was better left alone.

I was prepared for all of those things because if our relationship was going to evolve further, I needed to know the truth so that I could do something about it. I know that I am far from perfect and in order to create the relationship I ultimately want, it's important for me to go through this discomfort to get to a deeper level of connection. The willingness to apologize and acknowledge my mistakes in our relationship has been helpful in elevating it.

Did she say any of those things? No. Would it have mattered to me if she had? No, not at all, because I wanted only to know what was real for her. Any of my repair strategies would be based on her feedback and it would only serve our relationship.

She replied that I had not disappointed her and that she loved me and our relationship. Since that moment, from time to time I continue to pursue things that cause me discomfort that ultimately bring us closer together. She has responded again, and again, in ways that make me so grateful to have her in my life. We have had our share of difficult times and situations. Facing them honestly and openly with each other has brought us much closer together.

The greatest gifts that I have been able to give to clients have come from facing and resolving uncomfortable situations in my own relationship. The results of my personal relationship experiments have been incredible. My trial and error approach to figure this "marriage thing" out has been priceless. It has served me and others beyond my wildest imagination.

The random acts of courage have increased our love and connection. They have increased our passion for each other. The payoff of consciously bringing courage into the relationship has been the fastest and most effective way of achieving my vision. You can also choose to face the discomfort and find twenty seconds of courage. It might not only change your relationship, it might just change your life.

Summary

1. **Relationships need your courage.**
2. **If it was easy, every relationship would be inspiring.**
3. **You have the courage to do the thing that is difficult that will have the greatest impact on your relationship.**

4. Will you? Courage is a choice. It's uncomfortable. You can find twenty seconds of courage any day you choose to.
5. Courage gets easier and easier, the more you act with it.
6. The courageous act often results in the greatest pay off in results.
7. Expand your comfort zone often with your partner. Talk about and address the things that are uncomfortable because they have the potential to solidify and elevate your relationship.
8. Do something courageous in your relationship.

BONUS #2

The Number One Relationship Destroyer

People are great at relationship destruction; they do and say things to each other that they would never do to their good friends.

The Number One Relationship Destroyer— Derogatory name calling

One of the fastest ways to create resentment in any relationship is to call your partner a nasty or derogatory name. They are not easily forgotten. They are not easily forgiven. In my private advisory practice I have heard almost every mean, disrespectful name you can imagine. They sever connection; they destroy respect, and escalate arguments to levels of anger and frustration that are often difficult or impossible to recover from. Sometimes the escalation can result in physical violence to either partner.

Is it useful, or beneficial or helpful, to call your partner lazy, worthless, good for nothing, or loser? These are some of the mild ones. When you add the word *fucking* to worthless or loser it creates another level of emotional intensity. You can imagine the love and joy created when partners call each other bastard, bitch, asshole, etc, usually adding the word *fucking* in front of the word for effect. It happens to someone every day.

If this seems extreme, I assure you that some clients I have worked with have admitted calling their partner these names and far worse. These clients happen to be well educated, mostly affluent executives and business professionals, in case you were thinking that educated people wouldn't do something like this.

Calling your partner any derogatory name to friends is also something that is detrimental to the relationship because it shows a lack of respect for your partner. It doesn't impress anyone to tell your friends what an asshole your partner is because he/she did this stupid thing. The energy that you sustain in that act carries itself into the relationship, whether you are aware of it or not. The willingness to talk like that about the person you supposedly "love" and have decided to spend your life with sets an interesting standard for compassion and tolerance.

You cannot disrespect your partner while you are away from them and imagine that you respect them fully when you are with them. That's utter nonsense. It's not even remotely believable.

You want to destroy a relationship in record time, start calling your partner some of these names and see how well things work out. In the heat of an argument, most people have a preferred way of responding to hurt their partner. Survival instincts kick in and a particular word or phrase becomes a weapon of choice. It gets thrown out with devastating accuracy resulting in a correspondingly damaging response.

In the heat of an argument people choose how they react and respond to each other. It can get ugly quickly:

Remember that tone that you used in a response to a comment from your spouse? That brought about an escalated response from them, and then you reacted to that with some unkind words, and then they said something that caused you to say something you wish you hadn't, and then they said that thing you will never forgive them for, and now, any thought of intimacy with this person is met with disgust.

Imagine that you had the presence of mind to remember how much you loved this person and never reacted to any harshness other than with softness . . . how different would the outcome be?

You cannot sustain love in an environment of disrespect whether it's implied or spoken outright. Stay far away from the hurtful, derogatory name calling game if your relationship is important to you. Here again is another opportunity to choose. Choose wisely.

Summary

1. **Eliminate all derogatory and negative name calling immediately.**
2. **Eliminate all negative talk about your partner to friends and family.**
3. **In the heat of any argument remember why you love this person.**

Three Little Mistakes That Mess Up Any Marriage

What you don't realize you are doing can devastate the relationship.

Three Little Mistakes That Mess Up Any Marriage:

1. Taking Your Partner for Granted—Everyone wants and needs appreciation. Most couples think that the very fact that they are now married or have moved in with each other is a sign of commitment. The only commitment is what you choose to do every day to grow and sustain the love in your relationship. Neglect your partner and notice how quickly love dies.

In an ideal relationship, the children come second to the partner. This is another example of benign neglect, thinking that the children need me so I can't be there for my partner, he/she will understand. It's a great way to snuff the life out of intimacy. Date nights and couple time is very important not only to the relationship, but also to the model that your children will adopt for themselves. Make your partner the priority and give them the love and appreciation that they deserve.

2. Misunderstanding Communication—Men and women have different communication styles, and it leads to challenges. Men typically communicate in short direct ways, while women weave in more details and longer flowing volumes of communication. This can result in many misunderstandings and a loss of patience with each other's style. Individuals often jump to conclusions because they aren't actually listening to each other anymore.

When misunderstandings happen it's not unusual to hear one partner say that the other person just said something that they didn't actually say. I have witnessed this in consultations with couples and experienced it in my own marriage. One partner interpreted something in their mind that was not actually said, and they vehemently accuse the other person of saying it. It can lead to an escalating argument resulting in deep wounds. Both partners are certain that they are right, but one made a leap into non-truth based on previous arguments or defensiveness.

Words matter, voice inflection matters. The tone that you use with your partner is essential in avoiding communication misunderstandings.

3. Assuming Bad Intentions-Everyone makes mistakes, but the real challenges come when one partner believes that the other did something wrong intentionally. For example, *"I'm working my ass off and she only cares that there is money for her to spend, she doesn't care about me,"* or *"I've seen the way he looks at other women, he's not attracted to me anymore and he's probably having an affair."*

I mentioned a woman who called her husband "lazy". He didn't take it particularly well, understandably, but when we dug into the real reason for the comment, it had nothing to do with him. It was just a comment that came from her frustration about something else. When we assume that a partner intended to hurt us, or doesn't care, or is not interested, it often leads to bitterness and resentment.

Your partner forgot your anniversary, birthday, some other special occasion, or simply forget to run an errand, and you decide that they did it on purpose. Now it means that they intended to hurt you in some way. When you believe that, love, trust and respect all leave the relationship. It's impossible to trust and respect someone who you think is trying to hurt you intentionally. Your brain has a hard time trying to figure out where the role of love exists in that situation.

Always assume that your partner is human and prone to mistakes. Some are easily forgivable, and others not so much. Make sure that you give your partner the benefit of the doubt and know that your partner normally has positive intentions for you and the relationship. No one wants to suffer needlessly in a stressed out, bitter, and lifeless relationship.

We all have ways of trying to protect ourselves when we are hurt. Pay attention to what's in your heart, not the story you made up in your head.

Summary

1. **Make your partner the priority in your relationship.**
2. **Always assume a positive intention behind any undesirable behavior.**
3. **Your tone of voice often has more impact than your word.**
4. **We all make mistakes. Give your partner the benefit of the doubt where indicated.**

Meet My Needs

How much love do you give to the relationship?
How much happiness do you bring to the table?
How alive do you make your partner feel?

Meet My Needs—4 Needs to Care About

According to Human Needs Psychology, we all have the same inherent needs whether we are from the jungles of Brazil or the streets of Manhattan. These needs are universal. We share these same needs despite any perceived differences in ethnicity, culture, education, race, sexual affiliation or religious beliefs.

These needs drive us. They can make the difference between a loving, committed relationship and a relationship doomed to failure. Everyone gets their needs met. If you are not meeting the needs of your partner, they will be met elsewhere.

Have you ever felt that you were not getting your needs met? This is a great cause of frustration in many relationships. If your relationship is based on mutual giving and receiving, not only must you give, but ultimately you must get something from the relationship in order to feel like it has value for you. When we perceive that we are getting nothing back from our partners, we tend to shut down our own giving.

What do you need from you partner in order to be happy? What do you want them to do for you? This clarity is particularly important because if you don't know what you need from them, you will never be happy in the relationship. Lack of clarity causes suffering.

For the sake of simplicity, I will focus on four of the human needs:

Four Basic Human Needs

1. **Certainty**—The need for comfort, safety, security, and predictability.
2. **Variety**—The need for change, fun, surprise, adventure, and novelty.

3. **Significance**—The need to feel special, wanted, needed, unique, and important.
4. **Love/Connection**—We all share the need to feel love and connection.

Here are some quick questions to help you understand how these needs work in the relationship: *Answer them for yourself.*

How *certain* are you that your partner loves you?

How much *variety* do they give you?

How *significa*nt do they make you feel?

How much *love* do you feel from your partner?

The same questions can be asked of you.

How *certain* is your partner that you love them?

How much *variety* are you giving to your partner?

How *significant* are you making them feel?

How much *love* and *connection* do they feel from you?

Stop for a moment. You actually did this simple exercise right?

These four needs can be used as a gauge to determine how the relationship is doing. To be happy in your relationship, you must feel that your needs are being satisfied. In order for the relationship to be successful, you must satisfy the needs of your partner.

No one ever leaves a relationship when all their needs are met at high levels. There would be no reason to ever leave your partner if all of your needs were being met.

Here's an example of what I mean. It's time to put yourself in your partner's shoes for a moment.

Using a scale of 1-10, with a 10 being that you are meeting your partners need in that particular category at the highest level possible, rate yourself honestly to the questions below.

1. How *certain* is your partner that you love them and that you are always available to be counted on when they need you? How *certain* are they that they are the most important thing in the world to you? Rate how much *certainty* you give them on the 1-10 scale. ____

2. How much *variety* does your partner get from you daily, with fun, playfulness, laughter, pleasant surprises and new experiences? Rate yourself on your giving 1-10? ___

Too much predictability leads to boredom.

3. How *significant* do you make your partner feel? How important are they in your life, how highly do you value them and demonstrate that to them every day? How special do you make them feel every day? How's your rating on making them feel special 1-10? ___

4. How much *love* do you give to your partner? Particularly in the way that they prefer to experience *love* and *connection* with you? How close and deeply connected in their hearts do they feel with you? How loved do they feel by you 1-10? ___

How did you do? How highly are you meeting your partner's needs? Your honesty will reveal a path for you to improve your relationship. If you meet your partner's needs in these areas at high levels of 8-10, they will never leave you.

If you are meeting their needs at levels 3 to 5 or less, the relationship is struggling and you are not happy. Practically speaking the relationship is at risk.

While this may seem like a simple concept, it has enormous implications for the outcome of any marriage or relationship. What will you do with this information?

This is a great conversation to have with your partner, but only from a place of curiosity and learning. Not from a place of blame because you aren't getting what you want, or arguing about who is better at it giving. The conversation should be light, happy and fun. Laugh at yourself and then decide to get better at it.

I had this very conversation with my wife a number of years ago and learned a great deal. While I thought that I was doing pretty well, her ratings showed me that some of the things I was doing didn't have the impact that I had hoped they would.

Because I was curious about it, I didn't take it personally when I didn't hear that I was all 8-10s. I didn't defend myself, or argue with her grading of my efforts. I realized that if I wanted to do better, I would have to change my approach. This was completely my decision. The pressure wasn't coming from her for me to do anything. Our relationship was going great, but I wanted to know what was really possible between two people, so I made some changes in my approach. My vision for our relationship demanded it.

When you give your partner what they truly need, you will be surprised at what comes back to you. In my personal experience and in my practice, giving is the only way to get.

How highly are you meeting these four needs of your partner, and what will you do as a result of this exercise? *(Of course, you did actually do this exercise and put yourself mentally in your partner's shoes and rated yourself honestly right?)* This one thing cuts right to the core of whether or not you are being effective in meeting the needs of your partner. When you get it right, the relationship is filled with pleasant surprises.

Are you willing to have this conversation with your spouse? Are you willing to put yourself in a vulnerable position to hear that you aren't doing as well as you might expect and be perfectly ok with whatever that is? Are you willing to go first and take the responsibility to meet your partner's needs in the way that they prefer them to be met?

These are all just simple choices, easy to do, and easy not to do. Whatever you decide, know that the truth is this; *the difference will always be felt in the outcome of your marriage.*

Summary

1. Understand the four needs of *certainty, variety, significance, and love/connection.*
2. Recognize how well you highly you are meeting the needs of your partner. Is there room for improvement?
3. Understand what your partner needs from you and give it to them.
4. Talk with your partner from a place of curiosity about how to better meet their needs.

#5 BONUS

A Few Words on Affairs

Cheating and affairs are easy. What's the price people pay when their personal integrity has left them? What's the impact on their self worth?

A few words on Affairs—
When Men and Women Cheat

Affairs happen. Both men and women cheat at about the same rates today. The idea that men are the biggest cheaters is antiquated. Women have caught up and share fairly equally in affair statistics.

Affairs are one of the things that people turn to in order to fill an emotional void that exists in their lives. As you now know, your needs will be met inside the relationship or outside of the relationship.

Remember previously I mentioned that about ninety-seven percent of the time people do not end up with their affair partners. The fantasy of the affair is much different than the reality. Affairs can be overcome by a couple willing to explore the reasons behind it. Everyone gets to decide what's acceptable and what's not from their partner, as well as what they are willing to do about it . . . if anything at all.

Some people view affairs as a wake-up call and a chance to rebuild the relationship. Others believe that if a partner cheats, it's the ultimate betrayal and the marriage is over.

What are your rules about affairs?

What are the gray areas that betray trust? Is sexting someone outside of the relationship ok? Is having an intimate, intense, daily Facebook conversation with someone of the opposite sex Ok? Is kissing another person considered to be cheating? What about oral sex only? What about using escort services? What about constant use of porn? You get to define your rules around what betrayal and cheating mean for you.

What will you do if you find out your partner is having an affair or doing something that betrays your trust? Will you file for divorce immediately? Will you want to know all the details first? Will it matter if they are truly sorry and have broken it off? Will you ask if they are in love with the other person? What if it was a lust filled, one—time only kind of thing? What if it was with someone close to you? What if they beg your forgiveness and say they made a huge mistake and will do anything to prove their love to you? You get to decide what you will do.

If you decide to stick it out and work on the marriage, how will you know you can ever trust your partner again? Affairs are complex matters of the heart and head. They can devastate a family because often the affair partner is a known friend of the couple. What if it was with your most trusted friend?

Would the ultimate betrayal be learning that your spouse is having an affair with your best friend?

In my experience, an affair can be overcome when one partner is committed, and the other partner is open. There is no right or wrong about whether to stick it out and work on the relationship or not. That's your call. And that decision will be made based on the rules that you have about what the affair means to you. Is it the death of your marriage, or a chance for a new beginning? Is it the ultimate betrayal, or stress or alcohol driven stupidity? Meaning is everything.

Want to affair-proof your relationship?

When you treat your husband like he is your hero every day, and show your appreciation and gratitude for him, he is not very likely to want to have an affair. Find ways to value him in your life daily. How highly does your husband feel valued?

When you treat your wife like she is a goddess every day, and give her your presence and the attention that she deserves, she won't be interested in having an affair, either. Honor her in some way daily, and give her love the way that she prefers to experience it so that she feels connected with you. How deeply connected to you does your wife feel?

From my perspective, affairs are most often somewhat of a shared responsibility. I'm not suggesting that it's a fifty/fifty percent responsibility, but there is usually a reason a person has an affair that has something to do with their needs not being met fully by their partner. We all get our needs met one way (in the relationship), or another way, (outside of the relationship) as you remember from the previous chapter.

Re read the previous section to understand the impact of meeting the needs of your partner in the way that is most beneficial to them and your relationship success.

A FEW WORDS ON AFFAIRS

Affairs have never been easier. Plenty of people are willing and able to fill that role with your partner. There are services available to support affairs and cover their tracks.

The preventative solution is to meet the needs of your partner at the highest level possible and eliminate the reasons for them to get their needs met elsewhere.

Summary

1. **Affairs are widespread between husbands and wives at about the same levels.**
2. **Affairs frequently happen when needs are not met at home. The need will be met outside of the marriage.**
3. **What are your rules about affairs, and what will you do if you discover your partner is having one?**
4. **You can prevent affairs by meeting the four needs of your partner at the highest levels. Make your man feel like a hero, and make your woman feel like a goddess daily.**

The Four Levels of Relationships

You can live your life to never be rejected and protect yourself at all costs by withholding love, but you will never be happy.

The Four Levels of Relationships

There are four levels of relationships, and most people move back and forth between those four levels. What's most important is the level where you spend the majority of your time.

Level 1—Love is a Demand. You expect love, and your needs to be met on demand. If you don't get what you want, you get angry and upset. You are only interested in getting *your* needs met. You don't give your partner love or much anything else. Your partner's needs are irrelevant.

Level 2—Love is a Trade. If your partner does something for you, you will do something for your partner. You might even keep track of who does what for whom. In order for you to give something you have to get something in return. Sometimes you will do something for your partner with the intention of getting something that you really want later on. Maybe you have a hidden agenda. Do you ever remind your partner of what you did for them in order to get what you want? This is an exchange of giving; it is not giving to them because you love them.

Level 3—Love is Unconditional. You give love freely without obligation or condition, not needing anything in return. You give love because it is part of who you are. You give love because you want to share it. You give love to your partner because it makes you feel good when you do. Your partner's needs have become your needs. The needs of the relationship are also your needs.

Level 4—Love is Given When Hurt. You give love even when you are hurt emotionally. If you are a parent, you know that at times your children will do things that can be upsetting. You love and give to them anyway. Your partner can hurt you emotionally in many ways. You might love them anyway. This is the highest level of love, but does not mean that you accept abuse, or unacceptable behavior. Violence or any form of abuse is never acceptable.

Where do you tend to gravitate in your relationship? At what level do you have your relationship thermostat set? ____

Relationships that are at level one or two often struggle, because the partner's needs are met selfishly, and the other partner feels that they are giving and getting nothing in return.

When you are operating at Level three, your partners needs have become your needs. When giving freely to your partner, you are also meeting your own needs, and it feels good. This is the level that love and joy flow back and forth, where you experience love most all the time in the relationship. When both partners are meeting each other's needs regularly, the relationship is elevated to an incredible experience and is extremely fulfilling.

If you can love when you are emotionally hurt and remember how much you love them when things are difficult, that's an example of level four love. You take the higher ground and give your love no matter what.

Again, abuse is not acceptable in any form.

Summary

1. Understand the four levels of love.
2. At what level are you hanging out, and what are you going to do about it.
3. Abuse of any kind is not acceptable.

Re-Ignite Passion Now

Passion is the glue that holds the intimacy and aliveness of the relationship together, without it, it's only a friendship.

Re-Ignite Passion Now

When you were head over heels in love what was wrong in your life?

The passion between two people, the deep connection, sexual chemistry, and the desire for each other does not have to drift silently away. This does happen to most couples, but it does not have to happen to you.

We all live busy, hectic lives and if we are honest, we neglect our partners from time to time. We take them for granted. Yes, they do the same thing to us, but I will focus on what one person can do to restore passion in their relationship, that one person being *you* reading this now.

Restoring passion starts in your mind and actions. It will not happen by itself after three years without intimacy, no matter how much you hope and wish it was the way it used to be.

Here are four things you need to know:

1. **Have Courage**—There will be times when you will not want do what you are about to read. Your courage will help you do it anyway. It only takes less than twenty seconds of courage at a time. It takes courage to make something greater happen in your life.
2. **Make a Commitment**—If you want to create something amazing, you have to do something about it often. You can't go to the gym once every two months and expect to be fit. Commit to making these new ideas a habit.
3. **Be Clear**—Have a clear idea of what you want to create in your relationship. If you don't know what you specifically want, it won't happen. The more clear you are, the more efficiently you will work towards making it happen.

4. **Use Your Creativity**—The more you are willing to try new things and to expand on whatever is already working to create a unique experience, the more aliveness you bring into the relationship. We are only limited by our willingness to be creative.

Here are five steps to take now:

Step 1—Change your tone. Soften up and lighten up with your partner. Come from your heart and remember or imagine that you care so much for this other person. Really notice them and appreciate them for who they are. Let go of resentments and bitterness from the past for these moments. Drop any harshness from your voice. Soften your face and body.

Step 2—Initiate Connection While you have changed your tone, touch your partner more often, hold them, and kiss them. Bring more affection into your day to day routine no matter what else is going on. Engage them in light, playful conversation.

Step 3—Entice Remind them of things that you find sexy about them. Be specific, and tell them. Surprise them with an unexpected whisper about what you want to do with them. Allow that to sink in and percolate. Let it simmer. Be playful and fun. Passion is enticed out, it cannot be forced. Sensual teasing is good.

Step 4—Linger When you hug them or touch them or kiss them, maintain the connection for just a little longer. Take your time allowing the feeling to grow. Stay a little longer when you whisper in their ear. Hold your eye contact longer when you talk with them or tell them what you find sexy about them. Bathe yourself in these feelings of small connections that are building and heating up. Slow down, you'll like it.

Step 5—Surprise Everyone likes pleasant surprises. Create a habit of doing different things and exploring. Do something unexpected. Use your creativity to bring a new sense of aliveness to something that might be routine. Every moment can be different.

Do these things regularly and the chemistry and passion in your relationship will not disappear. It's far more likely to grow and expand. Imagine how you will feel in a passionate, deeply connected relationship. Imagine the aliveness that you will feel in these new moments. Bring more playfulness, fun, curiosity and adventure into your relationship. Start today because everything else can wait.

Summary

1. Passion creates an aliveness in any relationship and can be the glue that holds the marriage together when other areas suffer.
2. Pay attention to the needs of your partner. Entice passion out.
3. Have courage and be clear about what you want in your relationship.
4. Know how to ignite passion now with your voice, touch, playfulness, presence, and creativity.
5. Create new routines and explore the possibilities of passion with each other.

Summary

Relationships are like going to the gym and staying fit. Doing what works once every few months is not going to cut it.

Relationships are lost the easy way.

It's easy to neglect your partner. It's easy to make anything else more important than your relationship. It's easy to forget it's not always about you. It's easy to take it all for granted.

Most relationships suffer from a lack of vision. When there is nothing to aspire toward and work toward then everything else comes first. A compelling vision can unite and align any couple.

If the balance of masculine and feminine polarity that initially attracted you to your partner changes, then the intimacy and connection in the relationship start to disappear. Restore the core balance that existed when your attraction for your partner was at its peak.

You know that everyone needs to be appreciated and feel like they are understood. You recognize that not everything that you are doing today is beneficial or helpful in creating and sustaining love and passion in your relationship. You can change that.

You understand that someone has to step up if the relationship is going to change. That could be you. It's possible to have more heartfelt understanding for your partner. It's possible to remember how much you really love and value your partner when there is conflict. Will you?

No relationship is effortless and easy every moment of every day. People are human and we all make mistakes. We forget things. We often forget what's really important. We have good intentions and we still get caught up in the moments of stress, or upset, or overwhelm.

The reality of separation and divorce is rough. The emotional impact on your health and well being can suck the energy from you. The emotional impact on any children involved is brutal. The financial impact can be devastating.

People think they understand this, but *understanding is never experiencing.* Losing a relationship the easy way often brings long lasting pain and regret. The impact is usually much worse than people imagine.

If your relationship is not where you want it to be, you can understand this:

It will not get any better unless someone makes an active, conscious effort *to do something differently.*

The biggest mistake people make is thinking that things won't get any worse.

Nothing ever stays the same. The relationship is either growing in love, or losing love. The partners are either feeling more deeply connected or more separate.

Many people feel more lonely and isolated in a bad relationship than you can imagine. A miserable and even lifeless relationship can sap the happiness out of the partners. People can become numb, and fill their lives with insignificant busy activities to keep the emptiness away. The tread mill of staying busy to evade emotional pain is viscous and the suffering unrelenting. Most of us know people who are in this place.

People often mistakenly think they have tried everything to fix the relationship when it's not working. This is simply not true. We are all much more creative and committed when we decide that something is vitally important.

In my personal experience, and work with couples, there is one clear way to tell if the love and intimate connection in the relationship can be restored. *It takes one committed partner to step up and become courageous.* It takes one person to decide that they will do whatever is necessary. It takes one person to prioritize giving completely and selflessly to their partner, expecting nothing in return. This may not be what you want to hear, but it's what's true.

When one person puts the needs of the relationship ahead of themselves, it will only take a relatively short period of time before they know the truth about whether the relationship can be saved or improved or not?

It is of course, easier and faster if both partners are willing and committed to making love last with the each other.

Some people think that if they ignore the situation that it will magically get better all by itself. Pretending that everything is ok is a sure recipe for pain.

Remember when you were truly in love, what was wrong with your life? Everything was great. You were happy, and playful. Maybe even silly, laughing and joking around, very lighthearted because everything just felt good. Life just seemed to flow no matter what else was going on. You had this feeling of aliveness and excitement in your life.

But when you don't have love in your life and everything else is going great, you feel like something is missing. You can have exceptional financial, or business success, and a lot of possessions in your life that indicate abundance, but feel lonely and empty inside because you are missing out on that aliveness of love. We see it constantly in the celebrity world. The unhappiness wreaks havoc in so many personal lives. Fame and fortune are not enough.

You can be the most generous, caring, kind hearted person there is, and still not know how to communicate and understand your partner. You can be a billionaire with incredible levels of business success and not know how to make a love last.

If your marriage is lifeless maybe your excuse is that you have been married too long and this is just what happens over time. In fact you have proof, just look at your friends. That is BS! Maybe your standard for what is acceptable is too low.

There are plenty of couples out there who are in loving, committed, and passionate relationships even after forty or fifty years together. These people didn't just decide to be roommates, or stay together for the kids because the passion and intimacy was gone. In fact for them it's still very much alive and they are still head over heels in love. You can easily adopt a higher standard of what's possible in your relationship. You do get to decide that.

I hope you understand the hidden risks of doing nothing. Knowing that things should be better or that you should do something is impotent. The cost of getting it wrong will be tremendous on you and everyone else involved. Divorce and lifeless marriages take an enormous toll on everyone.

Make a decision today about the kind of marriage or intimate relationship you really want. Also make a decision about what *you* are willing to do to make that happen. You have learned some very specific strategies that will get you the results you want, but they will not work unless you actually do them. That requires a commitment, a willingness to pursue something better. Are you willing to make that commitment?

Remember, you have incredible power to influence your relationship, but the power to control no one. You can however control everything that *you* do in making love last. You can always control your part in the pursuit of a happy, deeply connected, passion filled relationship every day. It demands courage and a willingness that only a relatively small, joy filled percentage of the population have. Will that be your destiny?

Most people will never be truly happy until they get the relationship part right. It's that important. Decide today what you want to do about that for yourself.

To Those Committed to Love

What's your standard for love and passion in your life? Want an amazing relationship, then do something to make it happen. Don't just settle.

I believe that a successful, passionate, happy marriage is worth pursuing with nothing less than a total commitment because I have experienced the pain and regret of divorce. And, in contrast, today I know the fulfillment of having a truly extraordinary, deeply passionate, loving marriage. I also feel the freedom and peace of mind that comes from knowing exactly what to do moment by moment in my relationship. I want you to experience all of this magic. You now have the tools and strategies.

Some people prefer not to go it alone. If you would like to be considered as a potential private client, and are truly committed to your success, email me for a Complimentary Relationship Review. Email jeff@peakresultscoaching.com to schedule your consultation.

It would be amazing to make a "dent in the divorce rate," as my friend, Satyen Raja says and I would be honored and grateful if this book goes towards affecting that.

Love with Passion Now! Why would you ever wait?

For additional resources visit:

Website http://peakresultscoaching.com
Read my Blog http://peakresultscoaching.com/blog/

Follow me on:

Twitter https://twitter.com/peak_results
Facebook https://www.facebook.com/peakresultscoaching
LinkedIn http://www.linkedin.com/pub/jeff-forte-csic-cme/17/a41/2a3

Marriage Fitness Membership Group

Your Insurance For a Happy Marriage

Now that you have the key Breakthrough Strategies and Bonuses, it's time to put it all together to create the relationship success that you deserve.

Great marriages don't happen by accident. They happen because the individual participants do some very specific fundamental things regularly. This is marriage fitness. Actively working on the marriage is what produces the highest levels of happiness in couples.

You can choose to work on your marriage alone, or as a couple, and now you have plenty of tools and strategies from this book. As an alternative to doing it yourself, I want to invite you to join a private group of people who are all committed to creating extraordinary relationship success.

Because I can't work with everyone who requests my personal coaching, I created an affordable group program for anyone who wants to continue what they've learned in this book.

The Marriage Fitness Membership Group is designed to be a convenient way for individuals and couples to stay at the very top of their relationship game. It's a membership site where like minded people gather to receive valuable guidance and continuous support.

Here's what you get:

- ✓ You will have access to a private membership site with cutting edge relationship advice, private blogs and forums to share with other like minded members.

- ✓ Two 60 minute conference calls a month for live Q &A hosted by *The 90-Minute Marriage Miracle* author Jeff Forte and other Certified Marriage Educators who will answer your questions live. These calls are recorded so that if you can't make a particular call, you can listen at your convenience.

- ✓ Creative insights to address your most difficult challenges. You will have an opportunity to submit your personal questions anonymously.

- ✓ Ongoing reinforcement of what works. You will be able to listen and learn as live callers get their questions answered.

- ✓ Weekly tips to keep you focused and on track. Knowing what to do is great, but having the presence of mind to deliver what works in the moment is what matters most.

Marriage Fitness is similar to physical fitness. It's that constant process of going after what you want that creates extraordinary results.

The happiest marriages all contain rituals that keep them at an outstanding level.

Without attention and care, any great marriage will suffer and ultimately die. Remember, your marriage is either growing in love or losing love. You are either becoming more deeply connected or drifting apart.

Join Marriage Fitness today and continue your path to creating and sustaining an extraordinary relationship. It will help to ensure your marriage success.

As you know, there's a lot at stake here: your financial abundance, health and longevity, overall life happiness and success, not to mention the marriage model you provide for your children.

This low cost membership might potentially save you hundreds of thousands, or millions of dollars from the financial devastation of divorce.

Give yourself the best chance of having and sustaining a great marriage. Your happiness depends on it.

Keep Marriage Fit or Not. It's always up to you. Your low cost membership is month to month, and you can cancel at any time. For more information:

Go to peakresultscoaching.com to sign up today.

***Reference this book and get your first month free.

***As a special bonus refer a new member and get one month free.

***Special pricing for access to private coaching

***Inquire for Corporate Membership Pricing and Religious Affiliate Pricing